Financial Wellness Cinematics

AF887738

AUTHORED BY
SOURABH JAIN

penmanbooks.com

Penman Books

Office No. 303, Kumar House Building,
D Block, Central Market, Opp PVR Cinema,
Prashant Vihar, Delhi 110085, India
Website: www.penmanbooks.com
Email: publish@penmanbooks.com

First Published by Penman Books 2020
Copyright © Sourabh Jain 2020
All Rights Reserved.

Title: Financial Wellness Cinematics
Price: ₹299 | $10
ISBN: 978-93-90156-28-3

No part of this book may be reproduced or transmitted in any form whatsoever, electronic, or mechanical, including photocopying recording, or by any informational storage or retrieval system without the expressed written, dated and signed permission from the author.

LIMITS OF LIABILITY/DISCLAIMER OF WARRANTY: The author and publisher of this book have used their best efforts in preparing this material. The author and publisher make no representation or warranties with respect to the accuracy, applicability or completeness of the contents. They disclaim any warranties (expressed or implied), or merchantability for any particular purpose. The author and publisher shall in no event be held liable for any loss or other damages, including but not limited to special, incidental, consequential, or other damages. The information presented in this publication is compiled from sources believed to be accurate, however, both the publisher and author assume no responsibility for errors or omissions. The information in this publication is not intended to replace or substitute professional advice. The strategies outlined in this book may not be suitable for every individual, and are not meant to provide individualized advice or recommendations.

The advice and strategies found within may not be suitable for every situation. This work is sold with the understanding that neither the author nor the publisher are held responsible for the results accrued from the advice in this book.

All disputes are subject to Delhi jurisdiction only.

ABOUT THE AUTHOR

Sourabh Jain

The Volatility Coach
CIO Suskan Consultant

After graduating from St. Xavier's College, like any other young aspirant, I completed my MBA and CFA and went on a quest to secure myself a decent job and kick start my career. I was indeed lucky enough to get a Job during 2008 financial crises into ICICI Bank Treasury Department.

After serving Treasury of few Banks and NBFCs I found my learning curve getting saturated and simultaneously discovered that personal Financial Planning is a highly untouched area for masses and I can endeavour to channelize a Movement for benefit of the people – **Financial Freedom for all.**

That's when I opted to be a Financial Advisor.

I came across a Quote ***"People work very hard for Money but they fail to ensure that their Money works harder for them".***

During my short span of just 4 years I am ecstatic to have been recognised by **"The Economic Times as "The VOLATILITY Coach of India"** and we were recognised as **Most Preferred Financial Wellness Partner for Corporate by Sampark & PGIM India Mutual Fund.**

In the last 3 years of my journey, I am glad to have influenced the lives of 4000 plus people.

So, this is Me - out there to spread **Financial Wellness** among common man even no matter what ever is your income bar.

"We all Work Hard for Money "Is your Money Working hard for You!! You need to answer by yourself...

We usually have a tendency to delay our Financial Planning may be due to our Current lifestyle, lack of adequate knowledge or mere by our behaviour. We all remember dialogues & key messages from a movie. I have tried to link those with Financial Concepts to make the financial concepts very simple and interesting for the readers.

P R E F A C E

I sincerely thank God, My Teachers, My Family Members, Friends & My mentor Mr. Kanak Jain.

In the last 3 years, I have travelled across many cities across India into office premises of many Corporate such as Reliance JIO, Vistara Airlines, Titan, Kone Elevators in Elevators, Sony India, Kohler India, CESC, Bajaj Auto, Sodexo India and many more reputed Corporate with a mission to spread Financial Wellness among the employees.

This book is a compilation of my experience wherein we have interacted with thousands of people imparting Financial Planning & Wellness through unique innovative Gamification modes. ***The book reveals life changing story of 21 investors to whom different Financial Planning concepts have touch upon and help them imbibe financial discipline their life.*** *It covers entire financial planning journey right from how to plan emergency fund, towards planning insurance needs, wealth creation, retirement planning & distribution of wealth in a cinematic way.*

Relevance of Financial Wellness in today's VUCA World:

Today's Concern: It is observed that Financial Stress is the biggest challenge among the masses today, on account of rising lifestyle inflation, EMI & improper planning and lack of product knowledge.

Call to Action: In order to cater to the need we have taken an initiative of imbibing "Wellness through Financial Planning" among the masses through our innovative Games, Puzzles & Movie format.

Objective: When financial well being is complied the stress level rarely emerges among employees and in turn it enhances the productivity of the employees manifold.

I would also sincerely like to thank all the HRs of the respective organisation for understanding the importance of Financial Wellness and for taking an initiative towards employee-wellness programmes.

Also I am very grateful to all my investors for sharing their feedback & experience which has motivated me to pen down my experience in this book.

Award received for being recognised as The Most Preferred Financial Wellness Partner

C O N T E N T S

01 Are you as Fit as **Tiger** – Take a Financial Fitness Test

02 **URI** – Power Move and the Josh of it all

03 **One Idiot** Movie: Sometimes One Idiot is good enough

04 ENERGY CONSCIOUSNESS- **The Secret** way!!

05 Striking Balancing between **Zindaagi Na Milegi Doobara** (Lifestyle Expenses) **LAGAAN** (taxes)

06 A balancing approach is critical as we enter our Family Life – **Ta Ra Rum Pum**

07 **The Robot** : Multiply the Rajnikant Way – Power of Compounding

08 **DHOOM 3** - Samar or Sahir - Create your Own Financial clone

09 Have you Identified your Financial **LAKSHYA** (GOAL) of Life

10 **KAL HO NA HO** – Insurance Planning

11 Financial goals: Types and tips - Be focussed like **Milkha Singh: The Flying Sikh**

12 Be like **Rocket Singh** and learn to take calculated risk

13 Asset Allocation – **Khosla ka Ghosla**

14 Commit to investing – the **Wanted** way

15 Formula for Home Loan **EMI** Interest Recovery

16 Pay yourself First - **Return of One Idiot** unique message

17 **Chak De India** – Rebalancing Strategy

18 **Bahubali:** The Fearless Investor

19 **Dil Chahta Hai** - Where we Invest & where should we actually Invest

20 **Bazaar**: Learning the rules of the Financial Bazaar

21 **PK:** Our Behaviour Guru and Behaviour Finance

22 Cinematic Review

Chapter 01

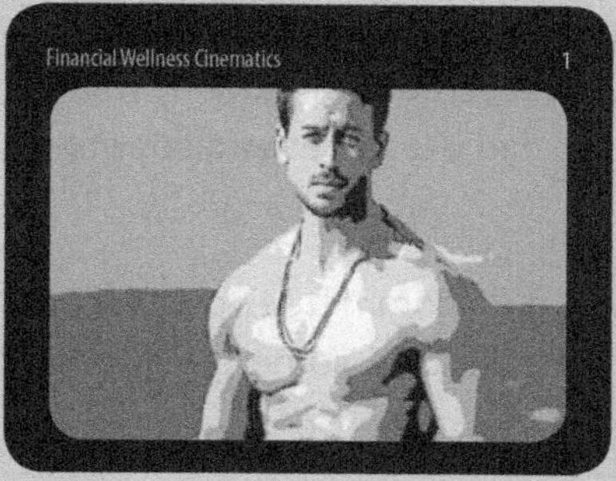

Are you as FIT as TIGER!!

We all admire Tiger for his fitness but it comes with lot of hard work, sacrifice & discipline - same goes with our investment...

Dear Readers,

Pretty much like being physically fit, achieving financial fitness is a process that requires your attention and complete focus. But what does it mean to be financially fit? It is the ability to cope with all your expenses and live your life the way you want, without any financial worries. For example, financial fitness will enable you to handle your loans, insurance policy premiums, monthly expenses and any unforeseen expenditure. It will also help you to create a plan that you can use to better deal with any financial need in the future.

Most of us are now focussed and committed to our health wellness. Some does gym, yoga, exercise some does walking and follow diet chart.

As Health Wellness requires discipline, commitment and some sacrifice, similarly Financial Wellness too needs these ingredients in terms of commitment towards regularly savings, budgeting & sacrifice in terms of few unwanted consumptions.

Financial fitness is a daily practice and requires consistent effort. It is living in a way that does not exceed income which we are earning and put emphasis on savings goals. It is making choices that are in alignment with priorities, and being disciplined with our wealth.

Before we start our Finamatic Journey : A small & simple questionnaire help us to identify our preparedness towards Financial Wellness Journey !!

ANSWER THESE FEW QUESTIONS TO KNOW YOUR FINANCIAL FITNESS.

1.	Do you have a Financial Plan in place?	Yes ☐ No ☐
2.	Do you save 10-30% of your take home salary?	Yes ☐ No ☐
3.	Do you have emergency fund to support for 6 months?	Yes ☐ No ☐
4.	Do you have adequate Term insurance?	Yes ☐ No ☐
5.	Do you have adequate Health insurance?	Yes ☐ No ☐
6.	Are you investing in a systematic & Disciplined manner?	Yes ☐ No ☐
7.	Are you investing for your Financial Goals?	Yes ☐ No ☐
8.	Is your portfolio balanced (Diversified)?	Yes ☐ No ☐
9.	Are you aware of the taxability on your investments?	Yes ☐ No ☐
10.	Do you review your Portfolio at least once a year?	Yes ☐ No ☐

Calculate the Number of "YES" and each "YES" has 1 point

Please fill as per your score: Out of 10 Your Score ..../ 10

As per your Score please tick the box :

0-2 Emergency, Start Soon. ☐

3-5 Alarming, Need to Plan. ☐

6-8 Healthy, Need some more effort ☐

9-10 Looks Healthy. ☐

This simple score will give us a fair evaluation about our current placement so that we can take appropriate action.

Key Notes from Tiger Fitness Studio

....

....

....

....

....

Chapter 02

Power Move and the Josh of it all

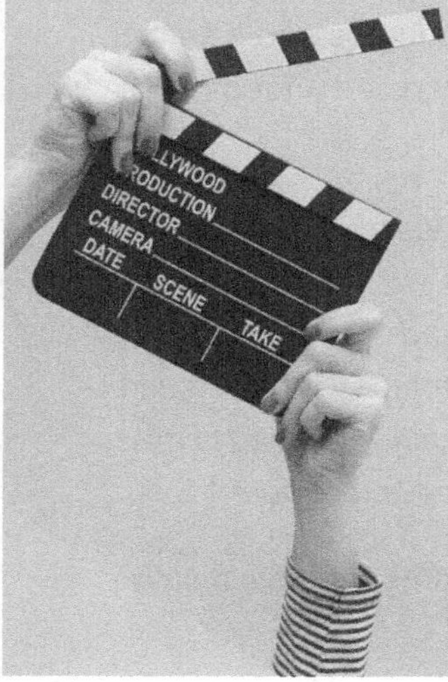

How's the Josh?

In our financial life, sometimes the only thing that is lacking is Josh. Our Power Move is all about that!!

"How much longer," my colleague Nishant quizzed the driver, the local man who was taking us to a Plant in Jhagardia where we were scheduled to run a 2-day session on Financial Wellness. Jhagardia is a sleeping hamlet, a remote town in Gujarat and around 3-hour drive from Surat. I confess that I was a little unsure about the place when we first stepped foot on it, but the moment I entered the Plant I was stunned by the well-managed premise.

So, today I had found myself at Kohler India's Gujarat Plant at Jhagardia. Kohler, as many of you must know, is India's top-notch bath fitting manufacturer. The HR professional greeted us warmly and arranged a cabin for us where we could conduct our presentation before all the employees.

I looked at my watch. It was 12 noon. "Let's start the proceedings," I told Nishant who, much like me, was a bit overwhelmed by this long journey and the entire surreal experience of being in such a remote part of the country. He nodded silently.

When spirits are down or when there is a bit of uncertainty about us (we were 2 strangers for these professional who watched us without much interest), we do what I call our 'Power Move'.

Now, '**Power Move**' is a prelude to our session and it helps to break the ice. Strangers no more remain strangers and a sense of solidarity is created. It also infuses in everyone a lot of *Josh* or excitement.

As we launched our Power Move, I addressed the audience, *"Friends, I request you to kindly stand with a straight posture like the army people. Roll back your shoulder and then count till 3. At the count of 3, you all need to yell at the top of your voice and perform any simple gesture or action. And finally, you need to give a high-five to at least 10 people of your choice in the room."*

They all stood up, some of them weakly and some enthusiastically.

It started.

"One, Two....and Three," the moment I finished the count, the room exploded. People forgot their mundane routine and gave each other a delighted high-five. Our Power Move had worked out beautifully. Then they were all ready to listen to us. Thus power move breaks the monotony of their daily unity work, unite them all and sets the platform for us to impart the Financial Wellness concepts in a very lighter way.

Dear Readers, let me tell you the real purpose of a Power Move. It is meant to break the everyday monotony and make the session feel more enjoyable. Our purpose is not to add pressure but to release that pressure. No session is complete if it cannot be engaging and offer freedom to speak, choose and express.

It won't be wrong to say that our entire session depends on the success or failure of the Power Move. So far, Power Moves has act as a catalyst.

Day 1 proved to be a great session as many employees signed up with us. Day 2 was even more exciting as now the employees were really looking forward to meeting us. We could do the financial planning of 30 employees in a single day.

Remember the famous line from the movie **URI – How's the Josh?**

Our Power Move is all about that. Putting Josh in the body and minds of all employees so that they are open and frank about their financial budgets, needs and goals.

We got very good response and employees explored our Financial Services. Mr. Gyanranjan immediately executed his plan after the session and kick start his journey towards attaining Financial Freedom.

Mr. Dalvi the HR processional was very impressed with the entire orientation of the programme and has referred us to few of the HR in his close contact. He specifically mentions that 2 mins POWER MOVE was powerful and set the stage for the entire session.

In our financial life, sometimes the only thing that is lacking is *Josh*. Are you ready to infuse it!!

Two Day Financial Wellness Session conducted at Kohler India - at Jhagardia Gujarat

Uplift your Josh from Power Move

Key Notes:

....

....

....

....

....

Chapter 03

Showtime One Idiot Movie

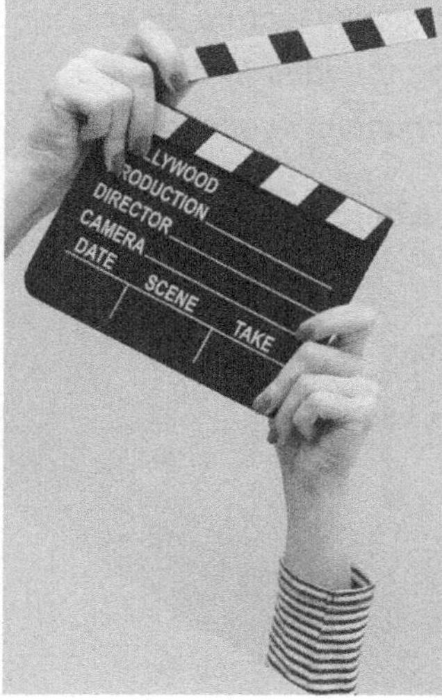

One Idiot Movie :
Sometimes One Idiot is good enough...

What does a movie give us? Entertainment, right?

But one evening on the dinner table, I was quite stumped when my wife put forth a question, "Can't you impart Financial Lesson through innovative means such as video or movies as people love watching these?"

It took me off-guard. I had never thought about it.

"It can be a revolutionary mode, you know," she added in a meditative manner, as if making a big prophecy about the future of this industry.

Next week, I went to check out this movie made by IDFC Foundation. It is called **One Idiot.** (Another incredible movie made by IDFC Foundation is titled **The Return of 1 idiot**). As I watched the movie at the plush Inox with a tub of popcorn in my hand, I realised that I had got completely absorbed in it. Even though the movie was largely about financial wellness, I had sunk into my seat in a cosy and enjoyable manner as if I am watching some Bollywood emotional flick.

It was an eye-opening experience. It made me realise that most people get bored if they have to listen to a preachy lecture when it comes to financial planning. But promoting the idea through a much delightful movie is a brilliant form of financial education.

Key Takeaways from the movie is briefed as below:

It's never too early to start thinking about money and never too late to stop thinking about money !!

Start as Early as Possible:

Be a bargain hunter for life:

Don't be impulsive in your purchases, only buy things that you do need...money saved is also money earned.

Investing tip: Buy investments as you would buy groceries, not perfumes!

Lesson 2: The earlier the better. The longer the better:

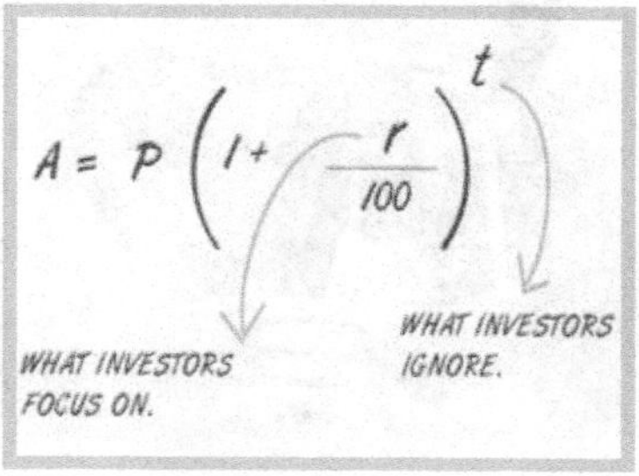

Lesson 3: Variety of shots to win the game:

1, 2 4 and 6s all required Winning a Game of Cricket... Similarly when it comes to investment we need asset allocation in terms of putting money into FD, PPF, Bonds & Equities.

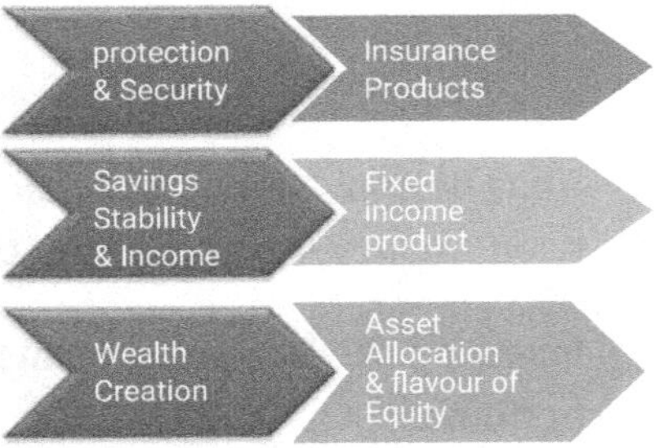

REMEMBER FOREVER!

Saving and investing is a lifelong process:

Don't be lazy and give up out of boredom or due to the pain of discipline and sacrifices (especially in the early years).

THE WORLD OF FINANCE GOES THROUGH CYCLES...GOOD TIMES AND BAD TIMES STILL...REMAINING INVESTED & CONTINUING INVESTING IS GOOD !

BUY LOW, SELL HIGH.... BE GREEDY WHEN OTHERS ARE FEARFUL...

BUY WHEN THERE IS A 'SALE IN FINANCIAL MARKETS'... WHEN 'THINGS ARE BAD'

Our sessions at Sodexo Corporate Office in Mumbai and at Kone Elevators in Elevators in Kolkata fetched us a marvellous response. The audience clapped and were really amazed with the experience as we showed the movie to them. Ms. Bhavika immediately signed up for Financial Planning and we helped her allocate her savings in Debt Fund, Equity Fund and International Fund. On the same day, I received a call from Mr. Ramchandra too and he referred us to his friend Miss Sejal. He had told me earlier that she often spends off a bulk part of her savings on online shopping. So, a savings plan can be a great way to ensure forced savings.

Our session at Sodexo was also a kind of an experiment for us. We weren't exactly sure how it would pan out. But the overwhelming response proved to us without a shadow of a doubt that we had hit the nail on the head with this concept.

I would sincerely like to thank Miss Harhita for sincerely following up in getting approvals for us to have the session at their premises.

Yesterday in my office, our newest employee (a 20-year old woman) asked a colleague Shahab to suggest a movie that she can watch at home over the weekend. Shahab's reply made me pretty happy and proud. ***"Watch One Idiot. The best movie for all the wealth seekers," he answered with a smile.***

I believe that you will now devote a few minutes of your life into watching this movie "One idiot". It can, after all, change your perspective. So, what's the big message you got from this movie? Do let me know.

For convenience purpose I am sharing the movie link:

https://www.youtube.com/watch?v=vU1l1TB7GzI&t=10s

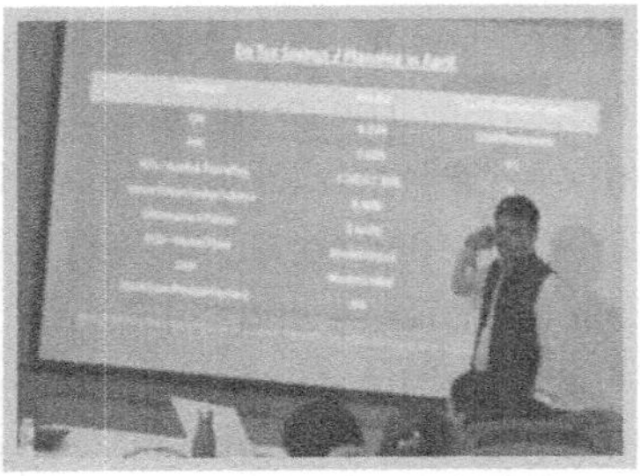

Financial Wellness Session conducted at Sodexo India, Mumbai Office

Was an Idiot good enough

Key Notes:

....

....

....

....

....

Chapter 04

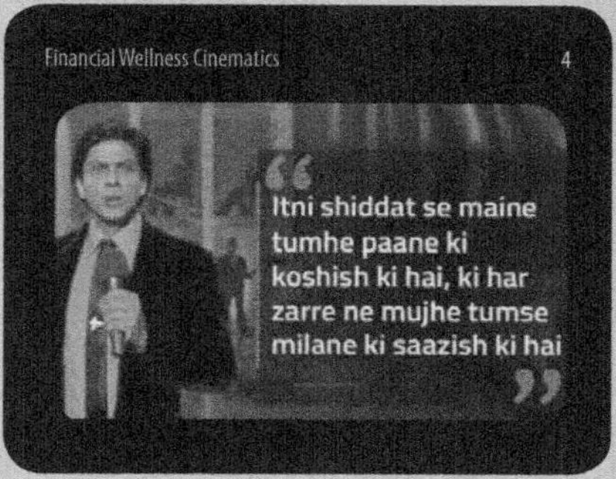

Money Mindset - The Secret WAY!!

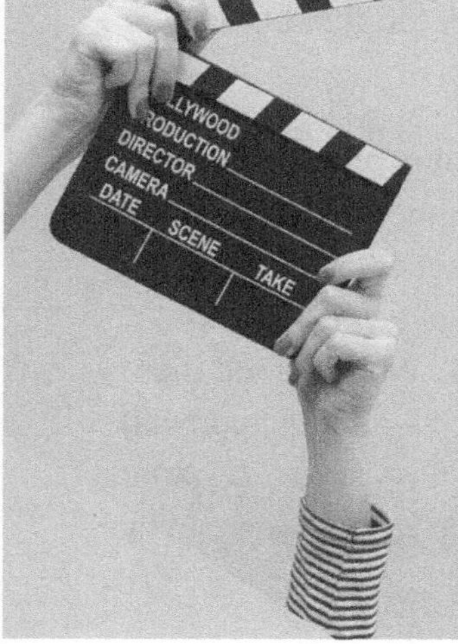

"Kehte hain agar kisi cheez ko dil se chaho ... to puri kainaat usse tumse milane ki koshish mein lag jaati hai"...

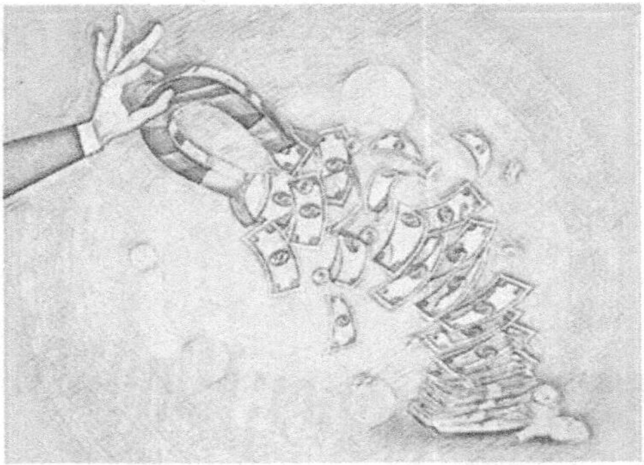

"Kehte hain agar kisi cheez ko dil se chaho ... to puri kainaat usse tumse milane ki koshish mein lag jaati hai"

English translation: It is saying that if you really desire something from the heart ... then the whole universe will work towards getting you that.

Are you the next person to imbibe the positivity of Energy Consciousness?

Attitude can break or make a man. Having a positive attitude and an optimistic financial outlook is another key to wealth creation. There are some people who have given money the label of a serpent or of a witch. They compare money to some evil omen and believe that a person who has amassed a lot of wealth must have done it through unfair and evil means. People having such a negative attitude never succeed in money matters. Even if money does come into their hands some day, it goes out the way sand goes out of your palm. They lose it all too fast before you can spell 'evil'.

During our Financial Wellness Session at Dabur office in Kolkata, I distinctly remember how we began the presentation by launching into the concept of money mindset. We often ask the audience our tried-and-tested question, "Have you seen KBC?" and the very obvious answer is a big 'Yes'. What we tell them (and most of them do nod their heads in agreement of approval) is that those who make such a windfall gain via lottery or game shows, often lose the entire or part of the pile within 2 years. Why does it happen!!

The same is also true for people in the Western Nations who rake in huge sums in game shows like '**Who Wants to Be a Millionaire**'. Education cannot be a factor here, as the winners in the Western nations are assumed to be more educated and literate.

But why did it happen to them too? Why 90% of them lose most of the money soon. As the discussion gained momentum and tea was served all around, Mrs Sarkar quipped, "They lose it all as they do not have a proper financial plan and they have spent the money on luxury." Quite right!

Another Mr. Dey prompted, "They should have taken advice of a financial advisor." We agree no doubt with Mr. Dey as well. All answers were along similar lines.

Since they haven't earned it the hard way and fortune has played an instrumental role in securing them the big money, they don't know what to do of it and often spend the entire winning amount (even if it is Rs. 1 crore) on extravagances.

However, as I made an added observation, "*The real reason why they are unable to multiply their Rs. 1 crore or even hold on to it is that they lack the MONEY MINDSET to do so.*"

Money Mindset as a concept is very appealing. ***Having Positive attitude towards money is the first step towards Wealth Creation. If you want to make more money we need to think good about it and bless people who possess it.***

Most of the people who won the money couldn't believe that this money belonged to them as they were not used to managing such money and their subconscious mind could not adapt to the change.

Thus it is always said that unless you dream big you will not be able to achieve it!!

SO the first principal towards Wealth Creation is to have a Positive Attitude towards Money. Very few Finance experts use such spiritual angle as the biggest vehicle towards wealth creation.

Most of the employees at Dabur India's Kolkata office displayed keen interest in the concept. However, they were unsure as to how can this bring them money.

"What does consciousness have to do with wealth creation," quizzed a lady by the name of Ms Sampa. "Read this book," **The Secret** I said, tossing towards her.

Thus having positive attitude about money is the first step towards Wealth Creation. The famous Book "The Secret" clearly reveals the power of subconscious mind. It is based on the belief of the law of attraction, which claims that thoughts can change a person's life directly. I urge all audience to either read the book or watch the 30 minutes movie version of the book "The Secret" in YouTube.

The concept was well appreciated as it gave a complete different dimension to Wealth Creation.

Over the next few days, we got to know Ms. Sampa better as we did her Financial Planning. She was 36 years old. We helped her kick-start an SIP in ELSS tax-saving fund, which seemed to be the most appropriate plan as per her income and age. She appreciated our approach and referred us to her friend Debanjan, a 45-year old professional working in one of the biggest Plywood Company of India. He didn't have any investments except for an LIC plan and a PPF account. After going through his income charts in details, we helped him buy a health policy and also start an SIP to ensure that he has diversified portfolio.

Our alliance with Ms Sampa has grown and she is our happy customer since past 3 years.

This movie has changed my though pattern about money management completely and would surely inspire all the readers to create positivity attitude towards money.

Are you the next person to imbibe the positivity of Energy Consciousness?

Are you the next person to imbibe the positivity of Energy Consciousness?

Key Notes:

....

....

....

....

....

Chapter 05

Striking Balance between Zindaagi Na Milegi Doobara and Lagaan (Taxes)

Zindaagi Na Milegi Doobara (Lifestyle Expenses) & LAGAAN (taxes)

ARE you a Victim of Life style Inflation?

Inflation vs. Lifestyle Inflation

Back in my high school days, the almost-adult child in me would often read without much interest (but merely to get through a class exam) that 'Inflation is defined as the persistent raise in general price levels of goods and services in an economy.' Back then, I had no inkling of the fact that the same term 'inflation' would form the backbone of a crucial chapter of my debut book on finances.

To get a perspective, let us cite examples from my own past and present-

Around 10 years back, the price of potatoes was Rs 4/kg. Now, it has jumped to Rs 20/kg.

We all are aware that price of commodities have risen over the years and, in all likelihood, will continue to rise. In other words, the value of money will fall.

But then there is something called **lifestyle inflation** as well.

I was on the metro train the other day when a child sitting on the lap of his mother said aloud, "Mummy, my school list has come out. I need a new pair of Nike."

It took me a few seconds to realise what he was actually talking about. And then it hit me hard that in our times, we would simply ask for a simple pair of black shoes. Today's child doesn't ask for "shoes". **He/she asks for a "Nike" or a "Reebok".**

Likewise, as a child I have gaped at Aishwarya and Shahrukh, paying only Rs 50 for a movie ticket and helping myself to a popcorn tub for Rs 20. Now, you need to shell out anything between Rs 120-1000 to get yourself a ticket and the price of popcorn tubs have gone through the roof (Rs 400 is what I paid the last time).

Consumerism has kicked in and we are no longer satisfied with a domestic vacation or with a budget hotel. Now, even an average middle-class opts for an international destination (Bangkok has become the new Digha/Puri for an average honeymooner). Resorts have become a habit and an annual subscription to a branded club has turned into a nationwide trend.

I managed to overhear another piece of conversation in that same Metro Train (looks like the credit for this chapter should go to that 35-minute trip I made down the underbelly of Kolkata Metro). This time it was a bickering couple. A demanding wife seemed to be bargaining with her husband about the car they should buy. *"Hyundai lenge please. Maruti nahi." [We would buy a Hyundai please, not a Maruti.]*

That got me thinking. I recall how back in the 90s the two-wheeler was every family's first choice (*remember the 'Humara Bajaj' jingle?)*

That night, I couldn't sleep well. My mind kept buzzing with thoughts. We have come a long way really. This is Lifestyle Inflation, where we have *chosen* to consume more, and we are competing with everyone else over brands.

For many of us, today definition of Savings is:

Income – Expenses= Credit Card/Emi

BUT now the time has come when we need to alter our Definition:

Income – Savings = Expenses

In my sessions, I often hear people grumble that they don't have the money to invest. 'I have nothing left at the end of the month. All goes into expenses and EMIs,' quipped one Mr. Ram Prasad Jha.

The millennial today are living their lives on EMIs. But we can kick-start the journey of SAVINGS if we are ready to alter our mindset.

Here lies the importance of Financial Planning.

I distinctly remember an eye-opening session I had with a lady named Ms Sharma. It was a part of a session (a session to discuss Inflation) I was conducting on Woman's Day in Bajaj Auto Pune Plant.

This is what Ms Sharma said,

"Prior to working in Bajaj, I had been working in Jet Airways in 2008. I was managing the Support function at the Jet counter. Naturally, we were used to overspending on luxury cosmetic products."

That's the lifestyle expense she had to incur (call it, a professional cost).

"Unfortunately," she added, "Jet was hit by a huge financial crisis in 2008 and a number of employees including myself was asked to take a leave for one month. However, nobody contacted us even after 2 months and we had as good as lost our jobs."

Taking a huge swig of tea, she added, "My savings got depleted in 3 months and when I phoned my mother to send some money, she asked me to sell off my belongings." Her mother, being from an army background, was a highly disciplined lady and wanted that her daughter manages her domestic crisis on her own.

"That year really helped me grow up - Financially. I learnt the rules the harder way. Now, I make sure that I save at least 20% of my monthly income. If possible, more."

Ms Sharma's resolution paid off as she was able to multiply her returns in just 7-10 years after opening a PPF & SIP in Mutual Funds. And let me reveal to you her age. She's only 29 at present. Pretty young, eh!

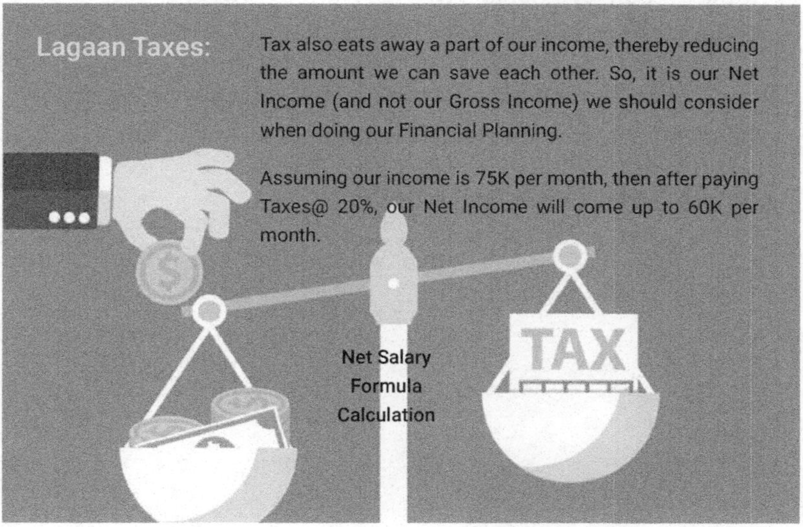

- **Net Salary (or Take Home Salary) = CTC (Cost to Company) – EPF (Employee Provident Fund) – Retrials – Deductions – Income Tax (TDS).**

So only after removing taxes and other components, one should start our Financial Planning.

Furthur, Tax planning is a an integral part of investment planning one needs to do Tax & Investment planning hand in Hand.

Instrument	Returns	Lock In Period (in Years)
EPF	7.55%	Until Retirement
PPF	7.10%	15
FD's – Banks & Post office	5.50 to 7.00%	5
Senior Citizen Savings Scheme	7.40%	5
Life Insurance Policies	5 to 6%	3-5 years
ELSS – Mutual FUnd	Market Linked	3
ULIP	Market Linked	
Home Loan Principal Payment	NA	NA

Note: A direct comparison may not be possible between the products due to their respective nature.

Rate may change from time to time.

"Women's From Savers to Achievers"- Session conducted in Bajaj Auto Pune Plant on Women's Day Celebration

Are you able to strike balance between Zindagi.... and Taxes

Key Notes:

....

....

....

....

....

Chapter 06

The story of a high-salaried corporate employee

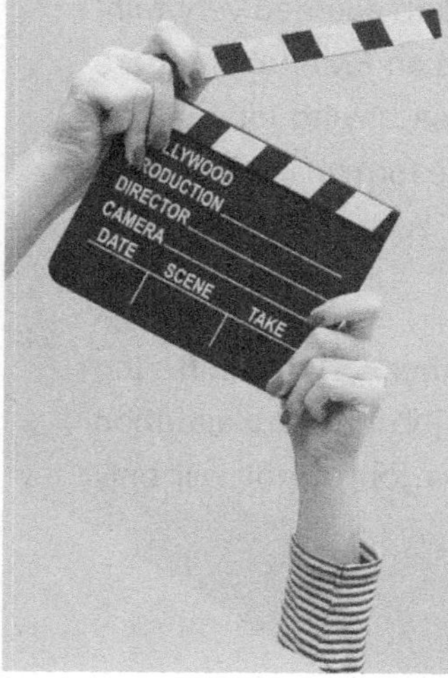

A Balance approach is critical as we enter our Family Life...

The story of a high-salaried corporate employee where wheel of fortune turned the other way: **A Balancing approach is critical as we enter our Family Life.**

This is the story of my friend Rohit, a Design Engineer working in Bangalore and having 10 solid years of experience in his career kitty. His story reminds me of a Movie Ta Ra Rum Pum which does not become the blockbuster but sets a perfect example of relevance of Financial Planning and avoiding unwanted expenses and being prepared for unexpected emergencies in life related to health issues, job loss etc.

Life was going smooth. But a time came when lady luck seemed to disown him. Organizational restructuring has become pretty trendy on the global level. Economic slowdown, growth of AI, cost cutting, improving operational efficiency and so on: the reasons are so many. But the solution is usually the same—employee Layoff.

The layoff storm hit Rohit too.

He kept trying for a new job in Bangalore itself for almost 6 months with no success. Since the layoff was due to economic slowdown, his chances of securing a new job seemed very thin. Given the mounting lifestyle expenses and an EMI-full life there in Bangalore, he was unable to accept less paying jobs either. Furthermore, most of his savings were in the form of illiquid asset such as Insurance product, PPF etc. and so he felt financially handicapped.

Staying away from home and family is another sort of a suffering we Indian youths have to combat. Losing a job in such a situation and not knowing whether you'll get a new job or not will only make it worse.

He had already stopped providing for his family in Kolkata. His home loan EMI back in Kolkata was being met from his investments as he didn't have an adequate cushion of emergency fund. As his savings further nosedived and fell below a critical level, Rohit made the hard decision of moving back to Kolkata.

The cost of living would be relatively minuscule in Kolkata as he won't be required to pay rent. Moreover, his expense would come down as he would be staying with his parents in Kolkata. He only needed to find that one job that fits and pays him right. It appeared to be a fair deal at that juncture.

But, was he in for a surprise? Would Lady Luck ever smile at him agan?

A couple of months went by as he struggled to find himself a rewarding job. Questions began to pop up in his mind as his confidence took a dip. It was the culmination of financial stress, fear of uncertain future, self-doubt and so many other things that sucked out his confidence.

"Did I commit a mistake by coming back here?"

"What if I don't find a job at all?"

"Almost half of my liquid assets have got used up in the past 7 months."

"How am I going to take care of my family?"

"How am I going to pay off housing loan and Gadget loans?"

"I cannot lose all my savings on this"

Here it becomes imperative to mention that Rohit had a lot more to worry about. Ever since he lost his job, he did not have any Term Plan and Health Cover. If any life casualty or health issue cropped up during this time, it would have become the worst days of his life. His family members would have to pay the debt perhaps by borrowing another debt.

Besides, his child was old enough to understand the ongoing crisis but was too young to be of any help. He was just in junior school. Rohit knew that he could not let any harm come to his child's education and the more he thought about it the more depressed and stressed he became.

After 8 months of joblessness and using up almost all of his liquid assets, Rohit accepted a job that paid him only 50% of his pay from the last job. He was literally forced by the financial crisis to accept a job that did not do justice to his worth.

What went wrong? Could he really have secured a better paying job?

Maybe or maybe not—the right job opportunities are only a matter of time. However, he obviously could have handled things better.

A few proactive steps that would have given better stability to Rohit:

- ✓ An Emergency Fund of 6-8 months of expenses would have given him the confidence and the control that he needed the most and lacked the most at that point.

- ✓ Every time Rohit reviews his portfolio, he regrets the investments made based on his friends' and relatives' advice which barely brought him 6% returns.

- ✓ *"It was a mistake that cannot be undone and I will have to pay the premium for the full term," he still laments.*
- ✓ *Rohit could have requested the bank for deferment of his loan until he got a new job and became financially stable. Considering Rohit's past consistent EMI payment records and his legitimate reason for inability to pay the EMI at that time, the bank would have definitely honoured his request.*
- ✓ *He could have invested a higher portion of his savings in liquid assets like mutual funds, FDs, Bonds etc.*

Basically, Rohit needed a strong financial plan that would have helped him to have a better life. Much better than the one he is having now.

Financial planning lets you know your financial potential and your limits so that you can take the right optimal decisions during times of acute financial crisis.

Unfortunately, he had to compromise with a lesser paying job just to manage daily expenses and keep everything afloat at home. This resulted in at least 5 years of setback in his life, because of which, Rohit is now compelled to change his financial goals and retirement plans.

Maybe if he had a financial plan, he would have stayed a little longer in Bangalore and found a good job. Maybe he would have negotiated boldly for a better pay. He would have had much lesser mental stress. Above all, Rohit would have preserved his precious peace of mind.

Here's the Big Question to all my readers:

If due to any circumstance, you are compelled to relocate or we take change in our job, how long do you think you can go without a steady income? How long can you provide for your family and fulfil your responsibilities? Do you believe financial planning could have spared Rohit some suffering?

It All Boils Down To:

The best thing about stories such as these is that they give us the heads-up. They give us the blue-print to prepare ourselves ahead.

Rohit are people like us—like you and me. It could be that guy who was sitting at a table adjacent to you in a restaurant. They have endured so much; some scraped out of the problem successfully, some are still trying to make it. A few share their experience with the world in the hope that someone would spot the issue at the right time and make ample use of it.

"The most important point in financial planning is that one must start early. A small amount invested over a longer period will have a big impact on one's portfolio. It cannot be compensated even by doubling the investment," says a financial expert.

"Creating a financial plan is not rocket science. You just have to put in some time and effort to ensure that the right ingredients are in place.

So, in the end, it boils down to two choices.

You may ignore what you have just read and carry on with your mundane and usual life, until one day YOU become the one sharing your story, only to become an eye-opener for the next person in the queue.

Or, you may start taking financial planning seriously and secure your life, while inspiring those around you for a financially better life.

Look! The ball is in your court now. Smash it or get smashed.

Strike a balance between your income and expense

Key Notes:

Chapter 07

The Robot: Multiply the Rajnikant Way Power of Compounding

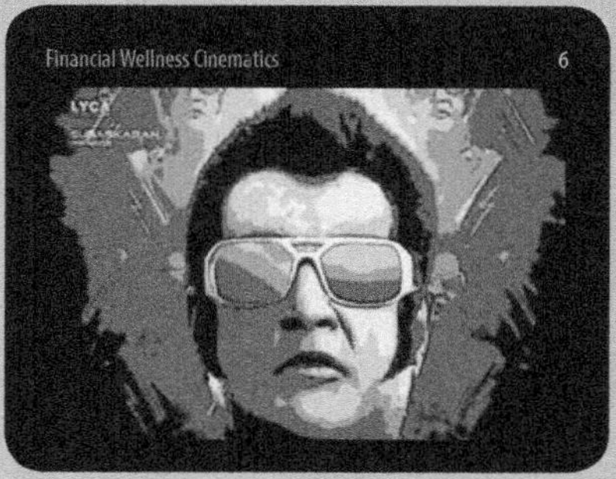

Robot: He was able to multiply himself into many Robots and increase his strength ; Similar is the effect of power of compounding to our portfolio that helps in multiplying our Wealth...

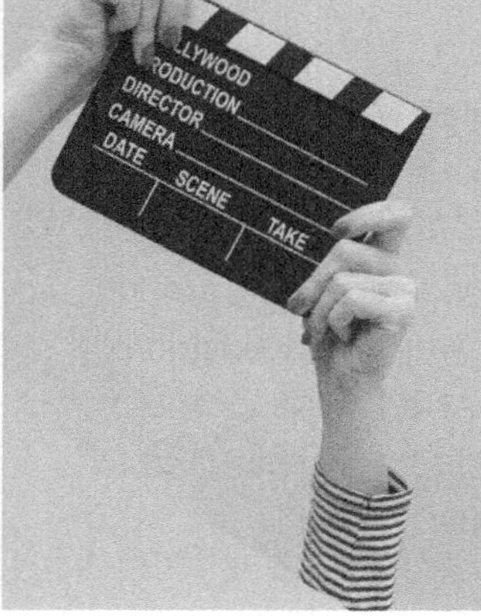

In the Movie: the Robot was able to multiply himself and increase his strength; Similar is the effect of power of compounding to our portfolio.

The Above Quotation is self explanatory:

This reminds me of a 26-year old guy called Mr. Sanjay Das a young profession working with Reliance JIO. He had been working at Rajarhat's Axis Mall Branch in Kolkata. An overenthusiastic man with a decent brain, I recall the way he was bouncing around like a ferret, answering all quiz questions with the precision of a sage at our Financial Wellness session. He was also one of those whose life took a turn (for the better) after we narrated to him the story of POWER OF COMPOUNDING.

Here's how the story goes:

There was a young boy in desperate need of an education loan. He approached the local moneylender, a *paan*-chewing middle-aged man with a fair amount of paunch. The moneylender looked at the boy from top to toe, spat the *paan* on the floor and said in a much scornful tone that he only deals with big businesses as his rate of interest was very high. He explained that his rate of interest was such that the money kept doubling every year. For example- the principal of Rs 1,000 would become Rs 2,000 in the second year and Rs 4,000 in the third year. And so on. The moneylender gestured to the boy to go away as it wouldn't be possible for the young lad to keep up with this rate.

The boy thought for a few seconds. Finally, he fished out a 1-rupee coin from his pocket and handed it to the moneylender, saying that he would come back later to recover his loan. The moneylender must repay him after calculating the amount at the same rate he charged from others. He accepted the 1-rupee coin and tossed it over to a small bowl he kept on his desk for quick change. The boy went away.

Over the next few years, the boy pursued higher education in Bangalore, secured himself a lucrative job, and became financially independent, settled down and then returned to his native town after 30 years. He remembered his deal and darted straight to the moneylender's house to recover his loan.

The old man, now in his early 70s, had become a very rich merchant by now. He recognized the boy and was pleased to see him making it good in the corporate field. The boy demanded his money back.

Here, I paused in my narration and asked my friend Mr. Sanjay Das to guess the amount the moneylender was to pay the boy. Mr. Das did a quick mental calculation and mumbled a figure.

Someone laughed from behind. A lady from the audience said Rs 6,40,000. But she was wrong!

Assuming that the Re 1 kept doubling every year, what amount would it reach at the end of 30 years? The amount is an unbelievably whopping sum of Rs 107 crores.

Years	Money (Rs)
1	1
2	2
3	4
4	8
5	16
6	32
7	64
8	128
9	256
10	512
11	1024
12	2048
13	4096
14	8192
15	16384

Years	Money (Rs)
16	32768
17	65536
18	131072
19	262144
20	524288
21	1048576
22	2097152
23	4194304
24	8388608
25	16777216
26	33554432
27	67108864
28	134217728
29	268435456
30	536870912
31	1073741824

Rs. 1/- invested on a day and money double every year - what is the vaue of investment after 30 years.

That's the beauty of **Power of Compounding**. Power of compounding is the key to creating wealth in the long term. If you keenly observe, after 8th year, the value of 1 rupee doubling comes to just Rs 64. But it keeps multiplying at an increasing rate and in the 30th year its value becomes Rs 100 cr.

We followed the above example with a real-life example of Mr. Ram & Mr. Shyam.

Benefits of starting early

The former made Rs 1.84 crore by investing only Rs 36 lakh, while Mr. Shyam built a wealth of Rs 95 lakh by investing Rs 45 lakh. In the end, both of them were winners. They had got a taste of the **Power of Compounding**.

Coming back to our story, the figure that Mr. Sanjay Das had mumbled out loud was correct. We gifted him a book. We also did Financial Planning for Mr. Sanjay and kick started his 1st investment.

He began with a small SIP with a view to cater to his Financial Freedom Goal.

Soon, he also realised the importance of having a Term Insurance Plan and he has recently covered himself with sufficient term coverage.

Our next target is to search for the next Sanjay Das? Who else can make it big by only investing a tiny part of his/her salary? Will that be you?

I would sincerely like to thanks Mr. Ashish Banka who was in the HR department of Reliance Jio Kolkata. He attended of our session in Conclave Club in Kolkata and gave us the opportunity to do session in 12 Branches of Jio across WestBengal.

Was Power of Compounding Powerful enough?

Key Takeaways:

....

....

....

....

....

Chapter 08

DHOOM 3 Samar or Sahir - Create your Own Financial clone

Amir khan's double role: It is the strength of two brothers that made their show A great Indian Circus show...

Similiarly create your financial clone to attain Financial Freedom

All of us aspire to attain Financial Freedom at some point or the other. We heard this caption in Social Media, Magazines but what exactly is Financial Freedom!!

" The day when our Active income becomes equal to passive Income = We have attained Financial Freedom".

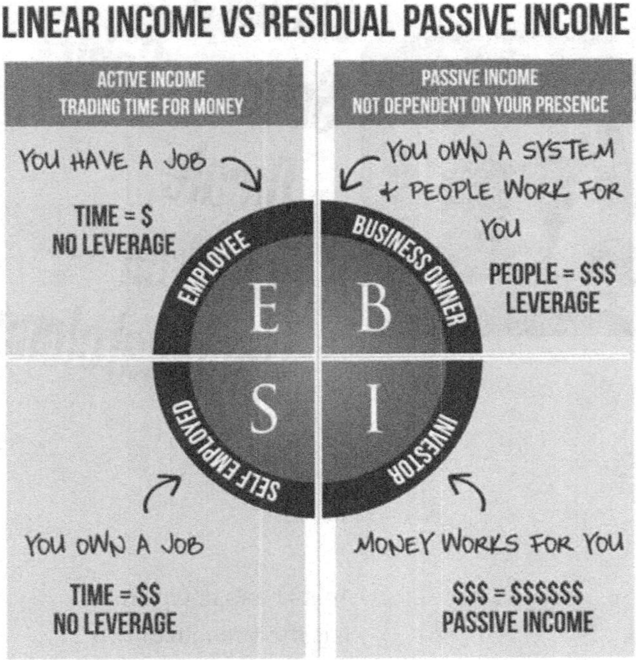

Once we narrated this statement in a session, question came from Mr. Prabhat an employee of Sony India working in Sony Patna Corporate office.

Could you please elaborate Active & passive Income!

I replied Yes!!

Active is sometime where we have to be actively engaged in an occupation either Business or Job. I asked Prabhat that you are employed in an MNC and you are earning salary. Suppose if you don't go to office for next 3 months will you get paid!

He replied no...

Then I narrated: 'Today I am doing training and earning my livelihood through my business. If I stooped this activity, will I get more clients and will I be making more money?

The obvious Answer is No!!

So this is what active income is all about. Be it an Entrepreneur and employer, if we not engaged activity we could not earn our livelihood.

This is what we call Active income – Our physical presence or involvement has to be there...!!

Now let's explore passive Income:

Let's take an example of a company like HDFC Bank. Today if MD of HDFC bank doesn't go to office the Bank will run smoothly. Entire operation is process oriented and is not run by single individual. So for an entrepreneur, in order to create a passive income he has to convert into a **big business and can earn passive income by receiving dividends & capital gains from his business.**

Similarly a salaried employee needs to create a passive source of income by saving a percentage of his income regularly. **An employee needs to diligently save and invest in a disciplined manner to create a passive source of Income.**

Ideally, if an employee SAVES 20%-30% of this salary = within

10 - 15 years he can attain Financial Freedom by making:

ACTIVE INCOME = PASSIVE INCOME

Let me elaborate the above Cash flow quadrant:

Cash flow quadrant is a powerful idea to achieve financial freedom by generating income through different methods. The cash flow quadrant divides the table into four, and each quadrant represents a different way to generate revenue. The goal of this approach is to follow the arrow and to gradually move on the right side.

However, to get rich, you don't need to shift completely to another quadrant. The possibilities are:

- ✓ Employee + Investor
- ✓ Self-Employed + Investor
- ✓ Employee + Business Owner

Also, keep in mind that each quadrant requires a specific set of skills. So before jumping into another one, make yourself competent enough for that quadrant.

Additionally, moving from one side to the other will be gradual and not an overnight process. However, the following steps are essential to achieve financial freedom.

- ✓ Make a long-term financial plan and set goals.
- ✓ Take control over your expenses and reduce debt.

- ✓ Identify the quadrants where you're right now and where you want to see yourself after 3/5 years. Start saving for your financial freedom journey. The earlier, the better.
- ✓ Learn about different investment avenues and their risks.
- ✓ Never get disappointed with mistakes, instead make them lessons.
- ✓ The most important one, believe in yourself.

Take the help of a planner for a smooth and stress free financial journey.

Prabhat got fascinated with the concept, and soon after the session, we had a brief conversation. But due to the shortness of time, we couldn't get into details on that day.

But to my surprise, he contacted me within a few days, and we discussed about his investment portfolio and spending habits. His then investment portfolio comprises of:

- ✓ monthly PPF contribution,
- ✓ one insurance policy, and
- ✓ A pension plan.

From the discussion, I realised that his portfolio is merely a collection of debt instruments that can give a maximum of 7% annual return, which is inadequate to beat the inflation. His equity exposure was zero at that time. He was investing only 10% of his salary. The balance amount of the earnings after meeting the monthly expenses and savings was lying in his savings account and fetching a return of 4% per annum. With the help of an financial calcuation, I explained the future value of his investments. Soon he realized that his investments are insufficient to meet his future expenses. The most significant fact I observed is that he was investing without a goal.

Hence, my first aim was to create an investment goal for him. **An investment without a goal is like a voyage sans destination.** By keeping in mind the details like his only source of revenue is salary (an active income), and his job carries a higher level of risk, I created a financial plan for Prabhat. The target was to develop a passive income in ten years by bringing his active and passive income at the same level. And, to achieve this, we proposed him to start a SIP which was missing in his kitty. He is very much destined to make his active & passive income equal in next 10 years.

Wellness Session conducted in Sony India Patna Corporate office.

Be firm and create your own Samar & Samir

Key Takeaways:

....

....

....

....

....

Chapter 09

Have you Identified your Financial LAKSHYA (GOAL) of Life

I could recall a dialogue from movie Lakshya
"Karan Shergill (Hritik Roshan): Romi, you always used to say that my life lacked any objective. Remember?
Karan Shergill: I have one now. [pointing to peak 5179] That is my objective.

Dear Readers, Please set up a time frame & attain Financial Freedom your Yourself.

Today, I would talk about what we label as the Financial Pyramid. A very recent memory takes me to the airport lounge of Kolkata when I had queued up to board my AirAsia flight to Mumbai. The flight was late by 2 hours and I chanced upon Mr. Mark, a middle-aged man and, as I learnt later, the sales manager at Telecom Company.

A chance encounter with strangers often turns into a small friendship and we open up before each other in a very frank way. Our conversation began as we both bickered about the flight delays that are getting more and more frequent. As I introduced myself as a Financial Planner, his curiosity piqued. He said, "Oh, I am myself very much keen to know more about financial planning. Just that I am unsure on certain areas and so I stay away from it." His fears and insecurities are nothing new to me.

SO I turned my laptop on and showed Mark this Diagram

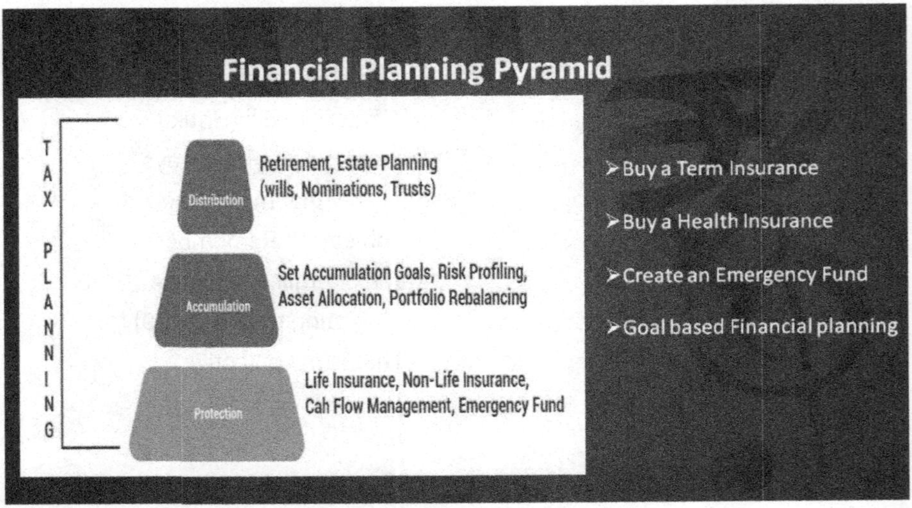

This Pyramid is a spiritual symbol of strength and energy. The base of the pyramid stands for the body, the sides show the spiritual attempts, the point symbolises the harmonious union of the human with the 'higher self-'(God). The base of the pyramid is like the base of any pillar, and needs to be strong so as to support the upper levels.

The Financial Pyramid, as can be seen in the diagram, is a three-tier structure. The base is the foundation on which any investor rests his funds for protecting himself and his family during situations of crisis. Such a situation may arise due to an accident, a disease, a sudden death or any such eventuality. The base, therefore, allows the investor to create emergency liquid funds which can be used during periods of emergencies.

The middle tier is of less liquid structure and it is also a phase that allows the investor to go a bit longer in his horizon. This is the accumulation phase, where an ideal investor would prefer to rebalance his portfolio. This rebalancing will certainly enable him to set long-term goals for enhanced capital growth i.e. capital appreciation.

The uppermost tier is a tier that gives the investor a space where he can think about his ultimate future and about his old age. Once the investor has fulfilled the needs for emergency funds and capital appreciation, he climbs up to the upper end of the Pyramid and decides to envision a retirement period for himself. By allocating funds at this level, he is preparing for a life after retirement. This is another crucial tier because it enables the young investor to start creating a secure post-retirement life for himself.

We got talking about the structure of the pyramid. Here is a quick overview of the discussion we have. I am presenting it in conversation form to help all readers get their queries answered-

Mark: This is all very interesting. Speaking of the base, I can see there is the Emergency Fund. But what is the ideal amount to be set aside as Emergency Fund?

Me: Ideally you should have 6 months of your monthly expense in your Emergency Fund. Supposing your monthly expense is Rs 20,000/. In that case, you should try to set aside Rs 1,20,000 [20,000x6] in an Emergency kit.

Mark: And what exactly do you mean by emergency?

Me: An emergency fund can be used at times when there is an:

a) individual emergency (like an accident or sudden loss of job or closure of business)

b) Civil or national emergency (the ongoing Corona crisis, being a fitting example)

In both such cases, you may not be able to generate fresh income during the said period. It is then that the emergency fund will come in handy. We are assuming that the emergency period should not last beyond 6 months.

Mark: Do we keep this Emergency Fund at home in form of liquid cash?

Me: Some amount can be set aside in liquid cash. But the money kept at home is idle money whose value decreases every year. Much better is to invest in Fixed Deposit Accounts or Liquid fund of Mutual Fund.

Mark: Mark made a mental note of all my suggestions. Munching on our sandwich and sipping on our steaming coffees, we decided to move up the pyramid. He was really surprised that so called financial planning can be explained through just one single slide and diagram.

He got enough clarity and could identify few blind spot which was not addressed be him earlier.

Mark's concern shot up greatly and he wanted a detailed review of his investment portfolio. I gave him my card and asked him to get in touch with me later that week. Over the next few hours, we became good friend and he was a gentleman and he convinced the person sitting next to me to swap seats with him. We discussed a lot more as the plane cut across the clouds.

Finance is a huge ocean and even a 3-hour flight journey is not enough to satisfy all queries. We shook hands at the airport as we exited the airport. It was a goodbye but with a promise of another rendezvous.

So dear readers, you too study the Financial Pyramid well and identify your financial Lakshya.

Make your Own Financial Lakshya

Key Takeaways:

Chapter 10

KAL Ho NA HO Insurance Planning

If a child, a spouse, a life partner, or a parent depends upon you & your Income- You need a **Term Insurance...**

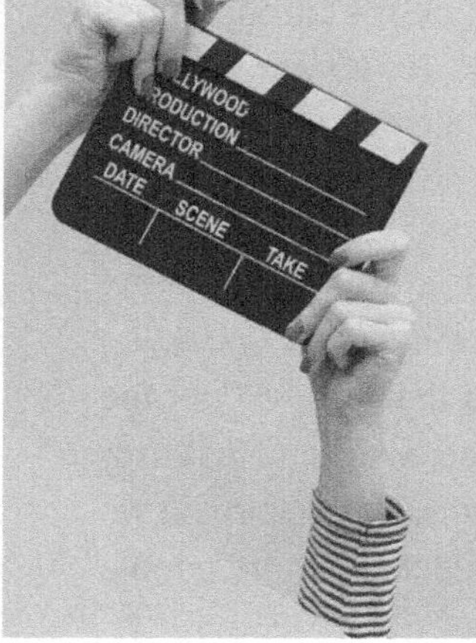

There's no tomorrow. Do it today. Do it Now!

The central idea of the movie Kal Ho Na Ho is very relatable for any person who delays in his Insurance planning.

Men often bond over a drink. I had one great conversation with a businessman some two years ago at a hotel restaurant in Mumbai. Beside Juhu beach, I was sitting on the restaurant table laid out beside the sea. The star-studded sky smiled down at me and the sea was making that soothing sound that makes us forget our earthly existence. As the restaurant boy placed a cocktail on my table, a gentleman came and parked himself on the chair beside me. Apparently, he too was on a business trip.

It was interesting how the conversation began. His name, as I learnt subsequently, was Ajay Tolasaria. A Marwari from Surat and a businessman with a couple of garment stores to his name!

After I introduced myself as a Financial Planner, he naturally began quizzing me on matters related to finance. And it is then that a very striking Indian mindset got noticed by me.

"I have an insurance that would fetch me around 15 lakh," he said, "for an annual premium of Rs 75,000."

It was a moment of pause for me. It struck me strongly that people don't treat insurance as insurance. They treat it as an investment and expect high returns out of it. I am talking about life insurance, of course.

For Motor insurance or Health insurance, people pay the premium without expecting any direct return. So, you keep paying the insurance for your car, knowing that you will get the claim only when accident occurs. Likewise, we pay Health or Medical insurance per year knowing that we will get claim on we are hospitalised or diagnosed with any disease. In short, people treat these insurances as true insurances- purely as a protection against a future hazard or contingency.

But the same cannot be said about life insurance.

So, I asked him straight and direct, "Do you think that Rs 15 lakh would be an adequate amount, given that you are paying a huge chunk of money as premium. In dire times, will your family be really satisfied with that amount?"

I familiarised him with the yearly rate of inflation and how the value of money falls by nearly 5-6% every year. I also pointed out that a decent return could also be expected from PPF account.

Therefore, treating insurance as an investment tool doesn't really make much sense, given that there are other better ways and modes of investing. Insurance, even Life Insurance, should be regarded as a pure form of insulating your life against death and seeking adequate monetary compensation in case of death.

Ajay's face fell. He saw the truth in my statement. He realised, to an extent, that he was not fully insured and felt a bit puzzled. "What should I do, now? You tell me, Sourabh?"

"See Ajay. I am not discouraging you. Neither do I say that you withdraw your funds from your ongoing plans. I am just saying that you should buy one more plan- a Term Plan, which will give you the truer benefit of life insurance."

"Can you elaborate a bit," he pushed.

"Yes, why not," I continued. "See, Term Insurance gives you better and more satisfying coverage. In case of death, your family won't have to depend on others. The only drawback, (which I feel is not really a drawback but many Indians feel it so), is that in case you outlive the plan, you won't get anything."

"Do you mean to say that if nothing happens to me, then the premium paid will be expense for me?"

"Yes Ajay. You may put it that way. But then when we go for car insurance, the same principle applies. Nobody minds the rules at that point. So, why not invest in your life?" I said.

This brings me to one of my sessions I was conducting at Vistara Airlines, Kolkata Office where I asked the members of my audience- "What is it that you value the most?"

Someone said, "My children." Others replied, "My parents." Some said that they loved their siblings the most. **But shockingly, none said that they value their own lives the most.**

Then I showed this image: Audience just gaze and Smile:

Yes my dear friend the answer is "YOU".

"WE" are the most important asset and we often tend to ignore it. The psychology behind it is that we take our lives for granted, believing that nothing could happen to us. That is why we fear for the lives of our loved ones. *As for our own lives, we are constantly living under the delusion that we will go on to live till we are really very old and then maybe we will die of our own free will (like Bhishma Pitamaha of Mahabharata).*

Coming back to my conversation with Ajay, he further asked,

"What is the idle coverage for Term Insurance? There is so much confusion as the agents throw at me 10 different choices."

I said, "The amount of term insurance that we should buy should be computed as our total annual expenses divided by prevailing FD rate for simplicity purpose.

For example,

Assuming Fixed Deposit rate is appx. 5.5%- 6% , if your total monthly expenditure is Rs 50,000 i.e. annual expenditure is (Rs 50000 x 12= Rs 600,000) then the ideal coverage would be 600000/6%, which is roughly equal to Rs 1 core."

Ajay was quite pleased to learn that there is a simple mathematical formula to find the ideal amount for insurance.

"There is a science to everything, even to insurance, my friend," I answered as I drained my glass of cocktail and ordered the food. It was getting humid by the time.

To my readers, I would give another example:

Option 1:
We buy an endowment plan of an insurance company wherein:
We pay 1 lakh premium for 16 years and at the end of 25th year we will get lump sum amount 51.25 Lakh rupees.
Return is appx. 6.5%
Life coverage is 15 lakh

Option 2:
Split the above 1 lakh premium payout into two components!!

Buy a Term plan for 1 crore = Pay premium of Rs. 20,000/annum

And Balance Rs. 80000 we invest per annum into PPF for next 16 years. For 8% years

Final Value of investment would turn out to be appx. 54 lakh.

Analysis:

In Option 1: We are having only Rs.10 lakh Life Coverage + Rs. 51.25 lakh final payout.

In Option 2: We are getting 1 crore life coverage: + Rs. 54 lakh at the end of tenure:

Now, the choice is for you to make.

Ajay further asked me, "And what about Health Insurance? Is any formula to get any ideal coverage, there?"

I said, "When it comes to health, one cannot put an upper figure to the cost you may have to bear once you land up in hospital. The cost of treatment can be anything from Rs 50,000 to Rs 25 lakh depending upon the disease.

But yes, I would say that opt for minimum health coverage of Rs 5 lakh and take top-up above it. Top-ups help to cut down your yearly cost, and still provide you with that additional coverage."

I showed Ajay, an illustration which is there as an image in my whatzapp:

A Rs. 25 lakh Health Coverage with a family floater feature come with premium of Rs. 36,000 per annum.

However if we split the same into 2 component by Buying a Rs. 5 lakh Basic Policy + Rs. 20 lakh Top up my total premium will come down to Rs. 20,400 only.

Thus we can save good amount of money by smartly buying a base policy and then doing a top up.

Ajay was really impressed with the illustration and all his doubts related to Life Insurance & Health Policy became absolutely cleared.

He further told me that none of this existing advisor has explained him the concept so clearly. Ajay took my card and to my surprise he called me after 15 days and executed his 1 cr. Term plan with us.

TO all the Readers

I believe Insurance is one such grey area where we need to invest based upon proper advice. One wrong decision can be very costly to our financial planning journey. Most of the time we have witnessed that a person's entire savings gets blocked in paying premium only, where neither he gets adequate coverage nor adequate return in portfolio to catch with the rising inflation.

Thus I would sincerely urge you to do your Insurance planning very effectively.

Session conducted at Kolkata Airport for Vistara Airlines employees.

Be proactive with your Insurance Planning

Key Takeaways:

....

....

....

....

....

Chapter 11

Financial goals: Types and tips - Be focussed like Milkha "The Flying Sikh"

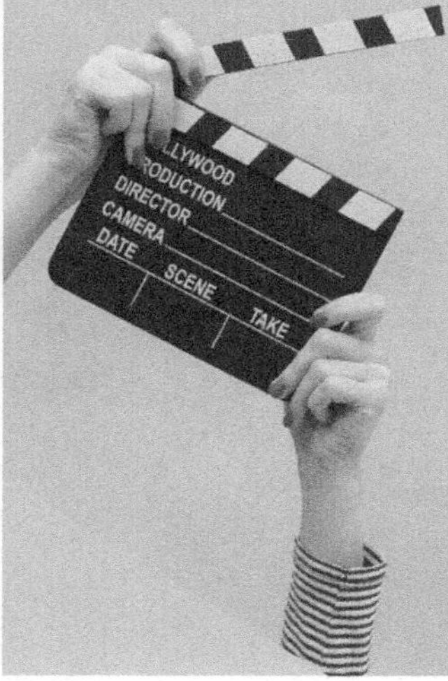

This movie motivates us to the core, to never give up and keep trying until success is achieved. Same Principal applied to our Financial Planning journey...

One of the most impressive lines I read as I was flipping through a financial book this week goes like this- *"An investor without GOAL is like a traveller without a destination."*

In other words, if you are doing financial planning but have not set yourself a goal or a target, then you will simply be wandering around like a lonely cloud in the sky. Creating a goal is essential for a much better financial health. Goals make your financial planning much more tangible, like a baby that you can mother or father and whom you can watch grow and become bigger and better.

We got a very Interesting assignment from Titan- to set up a Financial Wellness camp at their 12 branches on a single day. We took the challenge and our team spread across various Stores - Titan Eye, Titan Watches & Tanishq and we almost did one on one Financial Planning for more than 100 employees across 12 stores in a single day.

Finincial planning conducted for TITAN employees

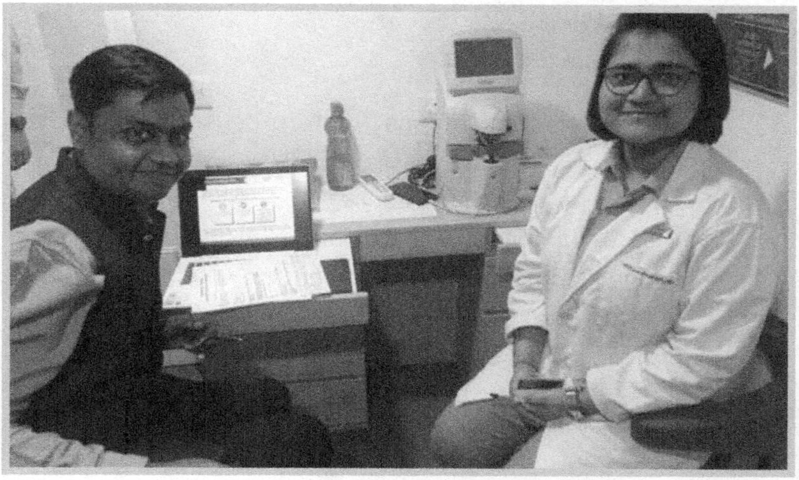

Financial goals can be clubbed and categorised into three main types:

Short Term Financial Goals:

- Making a contingency fund or emergency fund for family
- Saving for school admission of kids
- Saving for life insurance premiums
- Investments for tax planning. (Actually it's a mean but people think it's a goal)

Medium Term Financial Goals:

- Retiring a loan or debt
- Planning for a foreign trip or a vacation.
- Saving for college or pre college expenses for your kid
- Saving for starting a family in coming years
- Planning for a new or change of vehicle
- Saving for home/property investment

Long Term Financial Goals:

- Building retirement corpus (both, expenses and medical included)
- Saving for providing inheritance
- Saving for daughter's marriage etc
- Planning a home for post-retirement life or a farm house

Financial goals should be specific:

I want to become rich, is a goal but not a specific one. Here, you are being vague because richness has different parameters to different individuals. But if you decide that I want to build Rs 1 crore then your goal is specific and has acquired a visible and a tangible form.

Financial goals should also be measurable:

I would also like to emphasise the point that many people make concrete and specific goals and but do not give a precise financial measurement. For example, saying that you are saving for your daughter's marriage isn't enough. You have to give it a financial measure- like do you wish to save Rs 10 lakh for her marriage, or Rs 20 lakh or Rs 50 lakh.

While conducting the above sessions, we noticed that most of the employees are investing in some or the other instrument such as PPF, Insurance, Mutual Funds etc. But what they lacked is a GOAL BASED FINANCIAL PLAN.

I asked one of the candidates who was saving some part of his income to buy a house. In which year you wishes to buy the house and the locality where you would like to take it. This is for the simple reason that the real estate rates vary from locality to locality in an urban city like Mumbai or Kolkata and unless he gives a more specific measurable value to his future purchase, he may not be able to fulfil his dreams.

Financial goals should be achievable:

This book also focused on the idea that our financial goals should not be of dreamy nature but of a realistic nature. Just because you are planning a financial journey does not mean that you will dream of owning a jet plane. For instance, a person with a monthly salary of Rs 40,000 and a monthly expense of Rs 25,000 has his own limitations. He is, as visible, having a saving of Rs 15,000 monthly. In other words, he is saving Rs 1,80,000 in one year. Investments in Diversified Portfolio of Debt & Equity may give him a multiplier benefit. Expert advice becomes very, very crucial here.

Financial goals must be time-bound:

When I was in school or college, I used to tell myself that "I would complete this chapter soon. Or that, I would write this essay soon. But that soon had no expiry date." However, later in life I realised that one cannot be unclear about the time horizon here. When it comes to finance, you must set up your horizon so that you can see that future date when you will have your car and flat. For example- a time-bound financial goal will be **"I wish to buy a house worth Rs 50 lakh before 2030."** [here, you are setting yourself a goal in terms of material, measure and also time].

The session at TITAN was very enlightening for both the employee and for us. Our efforts were highly appreciated & we further got opportunity for to online session with their employees pan India during lockdown.

Dear Readers, I will leave you with some examples of Financial Planning which we did for the employees at Titan stores. We prepared holistic Financial Plan which includes plans related to Child Education, Retirement and their Children Marriage Plan etc.

Child Education Planning:

Sourabh jain
Sushant Rajput's Education Planning
rjaip@gmail.com
98366043882

Child Age	4 Year
Higher Education Age	20 Years
Current Cost Of Higher Education	Rs. 15,00,000.00
Inflation	4%
Current Investment For The Goal	Rs. 0.00
Return On Existing Investment	4%
Return On New Investment	10%

Based on above assumptions you shall receive

Future value of Education Funding	Rs. 28,09,471.87
Future value of your Existing Investment	Rs. 0.00
Deficit for which you need to Start Investing	Rs. 28,09,471.87
Option 1	
Lumpsum Investment require to achive goal	Rs. 6,11,422.93
Option 2	
SIP require to achive goal	Rs. 6,182.49

The plan above clearly specifies that Sushant need money after 16 years for the higher education. Current cost of Education is 15 lakh and after 16 years assuming 4% inflation cost would jump up to INR 28 lakh. Hence if Sushant save INR 6182 per month for 16 years into an asset class which yields 10% return he would certainly accumulate desired corpus of INR 28 lakh.

Ritesh Agarwal

Ritwik Agarwal's Marriage Planning

Child Age	10 Year
Marriage Age	25 Years
Current Cost Of Marriage	Rs. 25,00,000.00
Inflation	4%
Current Investment For The Goal	Rs. 5,00,000.00
Return On Existing Investment	8%
Return On New Investment	10%

Based on above assumptions you shall receive

Future value of Marriage Funding	Rs. 45,02,358.76
Future value of your Existing Investment	Rs. 15,86,084.56
Deficit for which you need to Start Investing	Rs. 29,16,274.21
Option 1	
Lumpsum Investment require to achive goal	Rs. 6,98,132.86
Option 2	
SIP require to achive goal	Rs. 7,261.26

Similar to child education we have created a plan for Marriage. Ritesh would get married after 15 years. Current cost of marriage is 25 lakh and after 15 years assuming 4% inflation cost would jump upto INR 45 lakh. His Father had already saved 5 lakh which would be accumulated to 15.86 lakh. Hence, additional 29lakhs is required and if Ritesh's father save INR 7261 per month for 15 years and if the investment yields 10% return, he would accumulate deficit corpus of INR 29 lakh in due time.

Like Milkha Singh learn to be focused towards our goal.

Key Takeaways:

....

....

....

....

....

Chapter 12

Be like Rocket Singh and learn to take calculated risk

Rocket Singh- Even Spiderman needs to take risk, I am just a common man There is a common saying, "Success comes to those who take risks in life." It is true that no one can accomplish their goals without taking risks.

FD vs Equity: A telephonic conversation:

An old friend of mine called me last week. I was lying on the couch like a cat, gaping at an interesting India-Australia cricket match. My favourite Rohit Sharma was on 28 and he seemed to be on a song. Fours and sixes were raining all around, when my mobile rang to my great annoyance.

It was my school pal Rahul and so I picked up the call. After exchanging greetings and discussing about our family affairs, he popped up a question, "I have Rs 3 lakh to invest. But I am puzzled- should I put it in FD or should I invest in Equity. Please advice."

His confusion is one of the most commonly prevalent confusions I come across in my sessions. As any financial advisor would tell you- FD does not beat inflation. Suppose, if the rate of inflation is 6% and the interest rate for FD is also 6%, you will still lose your money as you will have to pay taxes on your interest.

Again, it is a misconception that Equity is Risky. As long as you have a well-diversified portfolio, Equity is safe and even rewarding. On the other hand, FD is RISKY in the long run as it does not beat the inflation.

Coming back to the telephone conversation, I made a very saint-like quote that day as I told my friend, **"Dear Rahul, Equity is sometimes Risky in short-term, and FD is definitely Risky in long-term and vice versa."**

Let me explain to my readers in greater details and with an example:

For Short term if one Invests in Equity, Returns may go negative to the tune of 20% or more as we have seen in past but in long term even the worst 10-year average Return is close to 10% and the best is between 10- 15%.

If I invest Rs 1000 in Equity for 1 year and I lose 20%, I will be left with Rs 800 after 1 year. But if I invest Rs 1000 in Fixed Deposit Account @7.5%, it will become Rs 1075 after 1 year (assuming FD interest rate is 7.5%). If I pay tax @ 20%, I will pay Rs 15 as tax (20% of the interest amount of Rs 75). Thus, my net amount at the end of 1 year will be Rs 1060. So, in short term, FD gives safe and favourable returns as the compounded inflation factor does not hurt us much against equity which is volatile in the short term.

Here is HOW:

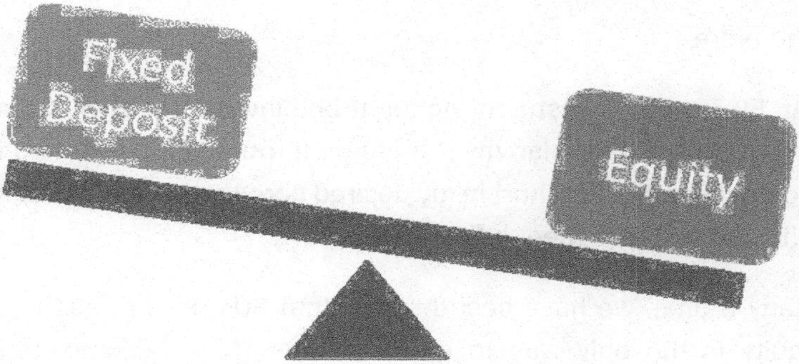

Rs.1,000 invested in FD

Rs. 1,075 @ 7.5%

Less Tax: Rs. 15 @ 20%

Rs. 1,060 after 1 year

Rs. 980 is the Real Value of Rs. 1,060

In the long run (say, for a period of 5-10 years), Equity gets you greater return and a meaty return. FDs will become dry. And what with the RBI cutting the interest rates, FDs are becoming increasingly unattractive.

Therefore,

"An FD is good investment option if one invests for short term goals. However if I plan my retirement through FD Investment I would definitely fall short in my desired corpus as in long term it will not be able to meet inflation.

Many a time, we have been hearing that FDs are useless and equity is the only way to create wealth. This is completely baseless as both products have their own advantages & disadvantages. Rahul was very satisfied with the explanation and this suggestion would certainly help him to execute his Goal Based Financial Planning using a mix of Debt and Equity depending upon his investment horizon.

" And with this final advice the, I hung up the telephone and went back to watching the India-Australia Match. Rohit Sharma was still there, now on 72.

Learn to take calculated risk

Key Takeaways:

Chapter 13

Asset Allocation Khosla ka Ghosla. Underscoring the importance of diversification

In the movie, Anupam Kher's character invests all his money in a plot of land. When the local goon usurps his plot of land, Anupam Kher's character risks losing all his money. This underscores the importance of diversification. Had he diversified his investments across multiple asset classes, then the adverse circumstances in one asset class, in this case the real estate that he had bought, would not had such a severe impact on his portfolio.

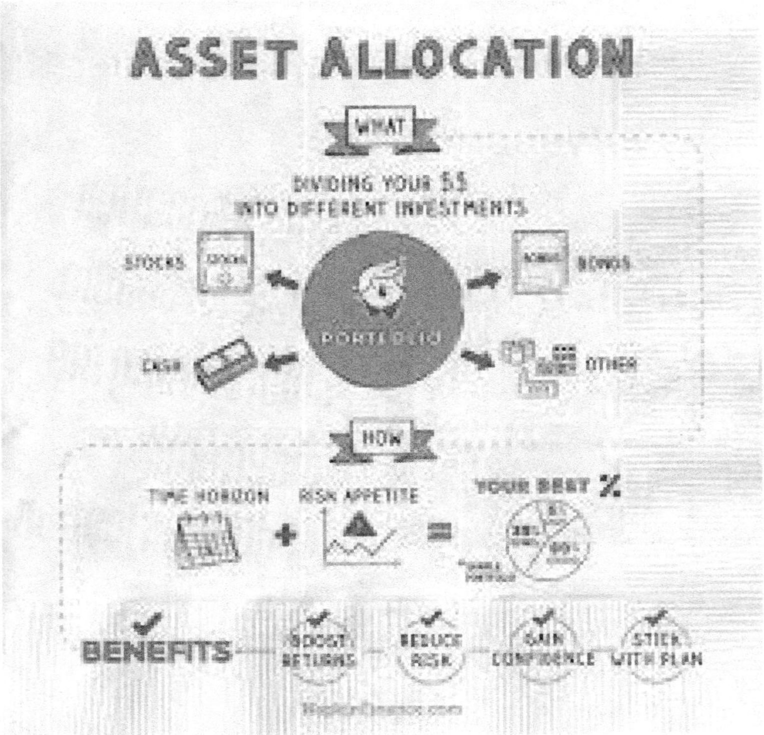

Before going into the details of asset allocation, here I would like to explain asset classes briefly.

Asset Classes:

Stocks, fixed-income investments and cash are the three main investment categories. Also, there are various subcategories for each one of these. A group of investment categories that behave similarly during changing market and economic conditions is called asset classes.

Risk and Returns:

Each asset class has its return potential and risks. Among all the asset classes, stocks have shown the highest growth and have given the most significant returns over fixed-income investments.

But at the same time, they carry a higher level of volatility and risks. This volatility is the result of the various market, economic, and business risk factors.

Asset Allocation:

To make your portfolio less sensitive to the wide swings in the performance of various asset classes, you should diversify the investment portfolio by investing in different baskets.

The process of including various asset classes in different proportions in your investment portfolio to make it diversified is called asset allocation.

Asset allocation is a crucial factor that determines the performance of your portfolio. Therefore, taking the help of an experienced planner is recommended for this. Depending upon your risk appetite, a financial planner design asset allocations for your portfolio by selecting the percentage of stocks, fixed-income investments, real estate exposure etc.

Selecting Asset Allocation:

While choosing an asset allocation, you should consider the following factors:

- The rate of return requirement,
- Your financial strength, and
- Risk appetite.

The rate of return requirement largely depends upon your financial goals. Your financial goals determine how hard your investment needs to work to deliver enough returns over the period to meet the goals.

So while setting goals, you should consider the current size of your investment portfolio and your ability to contribute to the portfolio in the future.

The time horizon also plays a vital role in determining how much risk you can take. If your goals are aggressive compared to your income and you have a shorter time horizon, then your risk-taking ability will be very less.

To summarize, I would like to say that the longer the time horizon, the more investment risks you can take. Also, don't forget to rebalance your portfolio to maintain the right risk level.

We conduct a lot of interactive sessions with prospective clients in different parts of the country. It helps me not only to educate the people about various investment options but also to understand different mistakes that people make in their investment journey. And I noticed that people of all age groups make a lot of common mistakes while selecting asset allocations.

In one such one on one session in Bangalore at Kohler India office, I met a middle-aged gentleman Mr. Abhishek. His portfolio was mostly a collection of stocks, as well as equity Mutual Funds. Apart from this, he was also having a couple of insurance policies that too were Unit Linked. I observed that his exposure to the debt instruments is negligible. I showed this slide during my presentation which clearly explains the relevance of Asset allocation:

The asset allocation quilt

The table ranks 10 asset classes in order of their return performance—from the highest to lowest—for each calendar year in the 10-year period from 2010-2019. For example, gold gave a return of 24% in 2010, and large-caps came in second with 17.43% in the same year. The absence of any pattern in the returns of asset classes from one year to the next reinforces the importance of asset allocation to build a portfolio against trying to consistently predict the next winning asset class. A diversified portfolio of stocks, bonds and physical assets is key to steering through every market condition. Such a portfolio may not deliver the highest return in any given year but will perform competitively across market cycles

2010	2011	2012	2013	2014	2015	2016	2017	2018	2019
Gold 24.00	Gold 29.00	Mid-cap 38.52	International 29.60	Small-cap 62.91	Credit risk 10.00	G-sec 15.00	Small-cap 59.64	Gold 8.00	International 27.31
Large-cap 17.43	Real estate 17.72	Small-cap 36.45	Large-cap 8.98	Mid-cap 54.69	Corporate bond 9.00	Corporate bond 12.00	Mid-cap 48.13	G-sec 8.00	Gold 18.00
Small-cap 16.69	Credit risk 8.00	Large-cap 25.70	Real estate 7.46	Large-cap 29.89	Mid-cap 7.43	Credit risk 12.00	Large-cap 27.91	Large-cap 5.91	Large-cap 12.65
Mid-cap 16.15	Corporate bond 8.00	Real estate 17.07	Credit risk 7.00	G-sec 17.00	G-sec 7.00	Gold 11.00	International 19.42	Corporate bond 5.00	G-sec 12.00
International 12.78	T-Bill 4.61	International 13.40	Corporate bond 6.00	Credit risk 14.00	Small-cap 6.10	Real estate 9.63	Credit risk 8.00	Credit risk 5.00	Corporate bond 10.00
Corporate bond 7.00	G-sec 4.00	G-sec 13.00	T-Bill bond 5.50	Corporate bond 13.00	T-Bill 5.38	International 9.54	Corporate bond 7.00	Real estate 4.83	Credit risk 8.00
Credit risk 6.00	International 0.00	Gold 12.00	G-sec 2.00	Real estate 11.91	Real estate 4.52	Mid-cap 7.97	Real estate 6.40	T-Bill 4.08	T-Bill 4.20
Real estate 5.50	Large-cap -24.64	Credit risk 11.00	Mid-cap -5.73	International 11.39	International -0.73	T-Bill 4.73	Gold 6.00	International -6.24	Real estate 2.60
G-sec 4.00	Mid-cap -34.19	Corporate bond 11.00	Small-cap -9.67	T-Bill 5.72	Large-cap -5.03	Large-cap 1.95	T-Bill 4.03	Mid-cap -13.38	Mid-cap -4.01
T-Bill 3.00	Small-cap -36.41	T-Bill 5.59	Gold -18.00	Gold 2.00	Gold -8.00	Small-cap 1.77	G-sec 2.00	Small-cap -23.53	Small-cap -8.98

Returns as of 20 December 2019; T-Bill: treasury bills, G-secs: government securities. For large-cap, we have used S&P BSE Sensex data; For mid-cap, S&P BSE Midcap data; For small-cap, S&P BSE Smallcap data; For T-Bills, CCIL Liquidity Weight data; For G-secs, CCIL All Sovereign Bond Index data; For corporate bonds, Crisil Corporate Bond Composite Index data; For credit risk, Crisil Composite Credit Risk data; For international, S&P 500 data; For gold, prices as per World Gold Council; For real estate, RBI House Price Index data. Source: Mint research

SANTOSH SHARMA/MINT

The above image clearly reveals that no asset class give consistent return year on year. In 2011 gold delivered handsome return and year 2012 was year of equity market which delivered 25% plus return across all Fund categories. Similarly 2105, 2016 were bad for Equities and Debt funds came as a winner during that year.

Thus what I am emphasising upon is that Asset allocation & Portfolio Rebalancing is the key strategy to generate wealth consistently.

Like in our lunch & dinner, we need combination of Rice, Dal, Chapatti, Papad and Sweet to satisfy our hunger. Similarly when it comes to managing our portfolio health we should have blend of Debt, Equity, Gold, and International Funds.

Hence, by keeping Abhishek income, financial goals, and time horizon in mind, I created an asset allocation for him. Various asset classes that we advised him to include in his portfolio are:

SIPs into diversified funds-

- Debt,
- Large Cap,
- Multicap Funds
- International funds

After the initial asset allocation, we periodically assess portfolio performance and does Portfolio Rebalancing for him.

Financial Wellness session conducted at Bangalore- Kohler India Office

Asset allocation is the key to wealth creation

Key Takeaways:

....

....

....

....

Chapter 14

Commit to investing the Wanted way

"Ek baar jo maine commitment kar di uske baad tho main khud ki bhi nahi sunta"

English translation:
"Once I commit to something... after that, I don't even listen to myself"

Discipline and Commitment are required to achieve our GOAL :

SIP in a nutshell: Everything you wanted to know about Systematic Investment Planning

Thus far, in our previous chapters, I have spoken about the power of energy consciousness. We have also sailed through the concepts of Emergency Fund, Term and Health policies and how to study the Financial Pyramid and move up the ladder gradually. Using simple mathematical formulae, I have also familiarised you with the Ideal amount needed for such funds. Now, I will talk about one of the most crucial elements of any financial discussion - **Discipline**.

Yes, my dear friends and readers- discipline is the key to a great investment. It is here that I would like to introduce the term SIP (abbreviation of Systematic Investment Plan).

What does SIP mean: **Investing regularly in a disciplined manner towards attainment of our Financial Goals.**

In one of my sessions at Techno Electric in Kolkata, I posed a very simple question before my 25-member audience, "How many of you invest in a disciplined manner? In other words, how many of you invest on a regular and a monthly basis?"

Only 5 out of 25 raised their hands, and I could not see many confident hands even there. I smiled encouragingly. One of my principles while conducting any session is to encourage people to open up to me frankly.

I said, "I am not unaware of your insecurities. People do not like to put their hard-earned money in funds and securities, since there is always the fear of loss, market-associated risks and the hesitation of parting with liquid cash. All of us do like to stick to liquid cash, as money in hand gives us greater confidence and makes us feel safe and secure."

I knew instantly that I had touched their nerves and many of them smiled weakly. Everyone could gauge the truth in the statement.

I continued, "See, the problem today is that most of the investors make last-minute investments during the months of January and February in order to save on tax. At times, their accountants, tax consultants or their own banks push them into putting their money in the available funds and stocks at that time of the year. However, by doing so, we limit ourselves and often make bad investments like picking up a wrong product which might not be matching with our Financial Goal."

I took couple of sips of water. The searing heat in Kolkata during the summer can make the throat dry even when you are inside a fully air-conditioned room.

Nonetheless, I continued, "The smart investor would not wait for the financial year to inch towards January before making his/her move. The correct thing is to invest through Systematic Investment Plan in a manner wherein you are not putting in too much money, and at the same time you are neutralising the ups and downs of the market."

An audience member by the name of Rajiv asked me to elaborate on the concept of SIP. My answer to him was, "Dear Rajiv, an SIP is like the Recurring Deposit account in a bank. You invest every month, instead of making one lump sum investment. And more importantly, you invest the amount you feel you can afford to invest every month. There is no pressure on you to make a bigger commitment than you feel is easily affordable.

For instance, I believe that each one of you can start with Rs. 2,000/ every month, if not more. It is a small amount you are going to pay out of your monthly salary every month. And this amount is not an amount that seems like a sacrifice. Just imagine yourself going on a big-ticket movie outing in a premium cab and ordering popcorns and cold drinks. Don't we spend Rs 2,000 quite often in such a 4-5 hour outing?"

Rajiv nodded and got the drift. Yet he, like many other members, wanted to know a bit more about different investment avenues and specially through Mutual Funds. **To give greater insight into Mutual Funds, I presented the concept in a single slide:**

WHY MF:

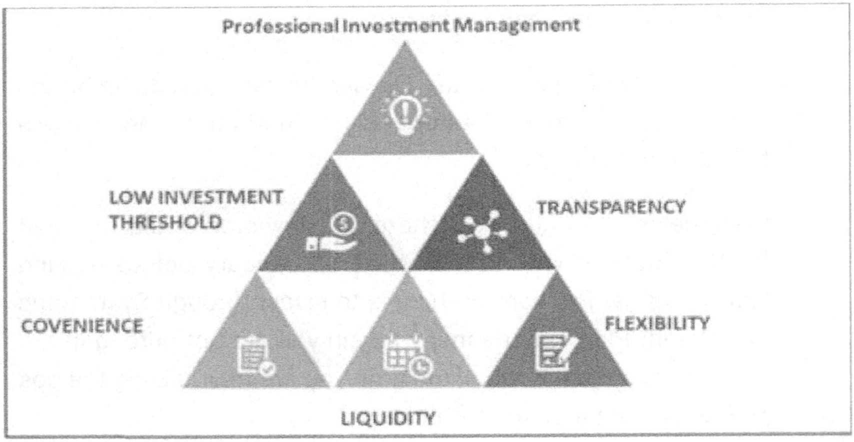

Mutual Fund: Fund Classification as per Risk Return matrix:

Before making any investment, Client must understand the Funds Category and is Positioning based upon Risk and Reward. **Liquid fund is the safest of all category and Sector Funds are the most risky**.

Mutual fund is

- Tax-efficient
- Relatively safer
- Gives you the flexibility to choose your investment amounts

and even change it anytime

- ➢ Easy to understand
- ➢ Offers you some of the best benefits of compounding

Fund Classification as per Risk Return Matrix

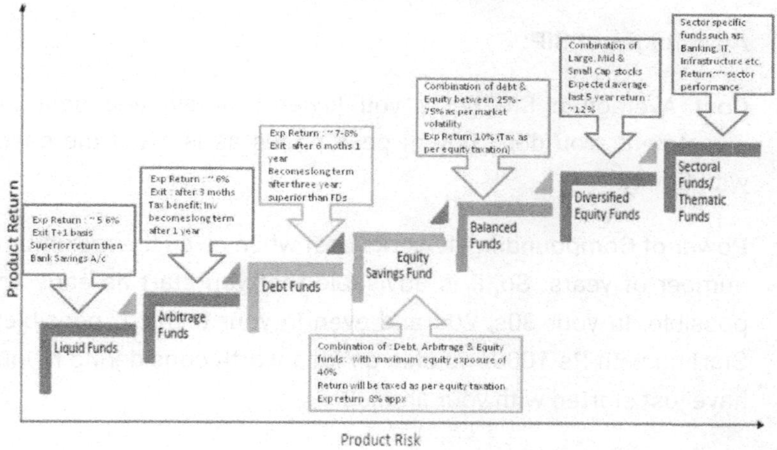

This classification simplifies the entire MF universe into one slide and gives a comparative view against alternative product available in the market.

For an investor who is looking for an alternative of bank savings account, Liquid Fund of Mutual fund is a better alternative where he can earn 5% interest instead of 3.5% in savings fund.

Similarly, Debt fund is an alternative for FD wherein investor can earn appx. 2% higher post tax return. But again with additional return there is an element of risk related to change in interest rate and credit rating of bonds.

Further, as we move up the risk reward ladder: one can invest in Equities for long term investing through systematic investment plan.

Mr. Das, a 38-year employee at Techno Electric, felt that it was an answer to his financial worries, as it sounded like a RD account where the investing amount is in her control and the compounded returns are rewarding.

Since a lot of people seemed extremely interested, I summed up the advantages of SIP in a nutshell:

Advantages of SIP:

Cost Averaging: SIP helps you lower your average cost of investment. You don't buy at peak prices as is often the case with Equity.

Power of Compounding: It works best when given the maximum number of years. So, it is advisable that you start as early as possible. In your 30s, 20s and even in your teens, if possible! Starting with Rs 1000/- is also an idea worth considering if you have just started with your first job.

Timing: Getting your timing right is of great essence. That said, it is not easy to do so. With an SIP, you invest across time, irrespective of the market timing. This increases your overall probability of getting your timing right.

Discipline: In an SIP, your investment process is automated. So, you never miss a single investment. Your financial goals can be met in your investment helping to inject discipline.

Small Investors: SIPs can be started even with the small amount of Rs 500 or Rs 1,000 whereas some mutual funds may have a higher investment threshold.

A young gentleman, Mr. Rajiv Questioned: Is SIP and (STP) Systematic Transfer Plan same?

No Rajiv it's not same:

An SIP helps you enter a mutual fund investment. But, what if you want to switch to another scheme within a fund family after you have invested in it? The STP or Systematic Transfer Plan may come handy here.

Say For example : I have invested in Debt Fund of HDFC Mutual Fund – named as HDFC Ultra short term Debt which is least risky fund primarily invest in Bonds having AAA rating.

One fine day, we see Equity market corrected by 5% on some global bad news. My Equity NAV is down. What could I do: I can switch some money from HDFC Debt Fund to HDFC Equity Fund to take advantage of such temporary fall.

Again out of curiosity - A person asked, "What Is Systematic Withdrawal Plan?" – The session was stretching beyond time.

I replied, "At regular intervals an investor is allowed to withdraw from your fund portfolio a fixed amount of money or units. Those who wish for a regular source of income this kind of plan becomes handy. The key requirement is that you have a sizeable portfolio of funds. Without that, you would not be able to withdraw any funds. An SWP helps you meet your liquidity needs. It is, therefore, usually used by retired investors as a pension. It is one the best alternative to Pension Fund as in Pension Funds we can never withdraw the principal. But here entire corpus is liquid.

The key advantages of an SWP are:
-No big capital gain tax
-Spreading of tax liabilities over the years
-Enjoyment of greater appreciation of funds

I wanted to end my session by explaining a very useful and easy-to-understand table.

With INR 2,000/- (SIP every month) we can be a millennial with time.

No. of Years	Total Invest-ment	PPF/ FD/Debt 8%	Balanced- Debt & Equity 10%	Equity 12%
5	1,20,000	1,46,954	1,63,339	1,63,339
10	2,40,000	3,65,892	4,60,077	4,60,077
15	3,60,000	6,92,076	9,99,160	9,99,160
20	4,80,000	11.8 Lakh	19.8 Lakh	19.8 Lakh
25	6,00,000	19 Lakh	37.6 Lakh	37.6 Lakh
30	7,20,000	29.8 Lakh	69.8 Lakh	69.8 Lakh
35	8,40,000	45.8 Lakh	1.28 Crs	1.28 Crs

** Returns are considered based on past trends

I ended the session by encouraging all the members to come out of their shell and experience the joy of financial freedom. "Kick-start the journey with a small amount! Rs 1000, 2000, 3000/. Anything you are comfortable with. But do it TODAY!"

WE got an impressive response after the event: We did the financial Planning of the audience members and helped them kick-start their investment odyssey.

So friends, I sincerely advise you to start your investment in a disciplined manner by making a financial plan for yourself. In the process, you will not only secure your future but you will stand a chance of becoming a millionaire.

Financial Wellness Session conducted at Techno Electric Corporate Office in Kolkata

Learn to be committed towards your investment

Key Takeaways:

Chapter 15

Formula for Home Loan EMI Interest Recovery

" Loan aur shaadi ek jaise hai... loan liya toh chukao, shaadi kiya toh nibhao":

English translation: A loan and marriage are similar... if you take a loan then pay for it, and if you got married then fulfill it...

It is an Indian mindset to own at least one flat, house or a bungalow. With women too getting into jobs on a full term basis, they too have become ambitious about owning homes in their names.

And here we come to one of my most curiosity-arousing slides, one that is often clicked by audience members.

Just to recall the last session in Bajaj Auto, I had on this- I quizzed the people, "How many of you are currently liable towards any loan?"

A mammoth, 20-21 out of every 25 hands shot up high in the air. In other words, at least 80% of the people carry the burden of one form of the loan or the other. It may be a car loan, an education loan, EMI payments towards mobile phones and tablets, and, of course, the big boss of it all Home Loan.

Home Loans can put a hole in your pocket if you do not plan well in advance. One of the major reasons why I made this statement is the whopping amount of interest you pay over the years. The ironic part is that in several cases, the interest amount gets too close to the principal. In extreme cases, it is also possible that the interest you pay becomes greater than the principal sum you clear.

In order to combat the demon of home loans, the monster-sized interest figures and the subsequent EMIs, here is a quick table/ slide that will give you an instant solution:

Loan Amount	₹ 40,00,000
Loan Term (in years)	25
Payment Per Term	12
Rate of Interest	8.5%
EMI	₹ 32,209
Total Repayment Amount	₹ 96,62,725
Interest Paid during the loan term	INR 56,62,725
Total Amount Required	INR 56,62,725
Investment Term (in years)	25
Payment Per SIP Term	12
Return Expected	11.5%
SIP	₹ 3,292
SIP as a % of EMI	10%

The chart is a clear indicator of how things stand. An SIP of Rs 3,292 only can help you to battle out the monthly EMI of Rs 32,209. The returns will be such that you won't have to pay interest out of your own sweat and labour. It is your own money (your investment, to be precise) that will do the hard work for you. **In mathematical terms, by just investing 10% of your EMI amount in the form of monthly SIP, you can earn the entre interest figure that you would otherwise have to pay from your pocket.**

The celebrated scientist and physicist Albert Einstein had said, **"Compound interest is the eighth wonder of the world. He, who understands it, earns it. He who doesn't, pays it."**

There is lack of logic and people can often take irrational decisions. A case in pointer is that of an old client Mr. Hitesh Jaiswal. He has a lucrative business and so he hardly keeps track of the mounting interest figures he is shelling out towards his new home. So, he purchased a flat for Rs 40 lakh and his EMI figure comes down to Rs 32,209 monthly. He had never really paid heed to it but it during a close scrutiny, I pointed it out to him one day over a mail.

"Your EMI and the term period reveals that your total payment will be appx. Rs. 96 lakhs. It means that for a loan of Rs 40 lakh, you will be paying a final amount of close to Rs 96 lakh. In other words, you will be paying Rs 56,62,725 only towards the interest. This figure is not just an astronomical figure but much more than the principal you borrowed."

It certainly had him interested. His jaws fell when truth hit him. I later suggested that he should start an SIP for Rs. 3292 per month. Taking that the annual return will be 12% on average (as per historic return) in 25 years, his investment would go up to Rs 56,62,725. It would simply mean that close to 70% of his entire home loan will get covered up by his investment.

Even though some people detest the idea of putting their money in the volatile equity market, mutual fund offers safety and security in the long run. This is so because you are then investing in a basket of stocks and the average return has been positive in the long run. It's hard to believe that a monthly investment of just Rs 500 for 35 years can yield Rs 97 lakh! It's true, and we are talking about average returns.

Financial Wellness session conducted in Burdhwan with few set of investors

Manage your EMI and simultaneously save for your long term goal

Key Takeaways:

Chapter 16

Showtime again. Return of One Idiot

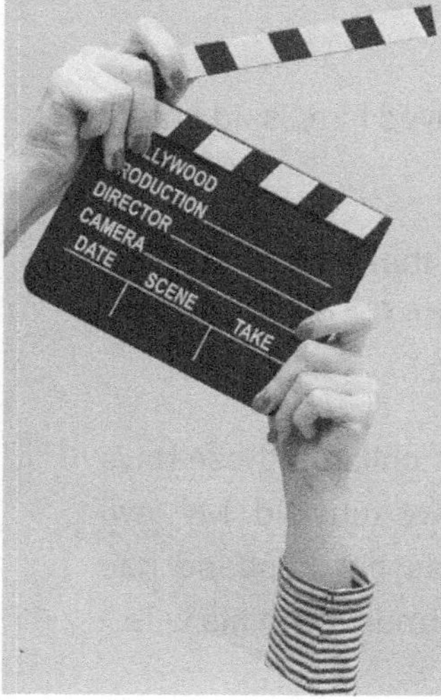

Return of One Idiot: All about of your Retirement Planning...

Pay yourself First - Return of One Idiot's unique message:

Will you be forced to work at 77 to earn your bread and tea?

"Today, I would like to cite the example of another movie, **Return of One Idiot.** *It is another inspiring and heart-winning short film and a sequel to One Idiot (about which I have spoken in one of my previous chapters).*

To sum it up, this movie is a poignant portrayal of the life of a taxi driver. It is about his journey from youth to old age and how he earns his living at the age of 77 by driving a taxi. He feeds and looks after his family throughout his life. But the sad part is when he crosses the age of 60 and becomes weak and old; he is compelled to drive a taxi. It is painful to watch an old, tired man forced to run a cab at an age when he should have retired and be at peace with life. But the reason why he has to go on with his work is that he needed money to survive. At the age of 77! Yes, even then!"

When I narrated this in one of my sessions where I was supposed to give a session on Importance of retirement planning!, There followed a pin-drop silence. People were moved and felt that life hadn't done justice with him.

"What was his fault then? His children betrayed him," said one of the men from the audience.

"His fault, my dear friend," I answered, "was that he did not make a retirement plan. He did not set aside funds for his own future self, but he relied completely on his children."

Another person commented, "It is true that children these days cannot be counted to look after us when we turn old. My own aunt now stays alone in her apartment as her husband has passed away and her son has shifted to Germany with his wife."

Moral of the Story: You need to chalk out a Retirement planning when you are young so that you do not regret when you are old.

As I was flying back to Kolkata a couple of days later, it struck me that why we do this to our parents. I kept myself in that position and asked myself if I could ever do so with my parents. The answer that came from my heart was a big NO.

And then I asked myself another question, "Saurabh, do you think that your child can do this to you thirty years from now?"

Somehow I felt I wasn't sure. Like the bird in the nest, they may also fly away one day in search of JOB, leaving me behind grappling with my loneliness in my old age.

The first thing I did when I reached home is parking separate funds dedicated towards my retirement. This was the only major plan that was missing from my own kitty, as I had always felt that 'what's the need of saving too much for the future when I have my good children.'

But that day, I just couldn't be sure. Even today, I am not. Are you?

To all my young readers:

Throughout our life we keep on planning something for our family members: Either for child education, marriage, business setup, meeting family member health care needs etc.

But somewhere in the race we always forget ourselves!!

"Robert Kiyosaki in his book Rich Dad Poor Dad narrated " Pay yourself first"

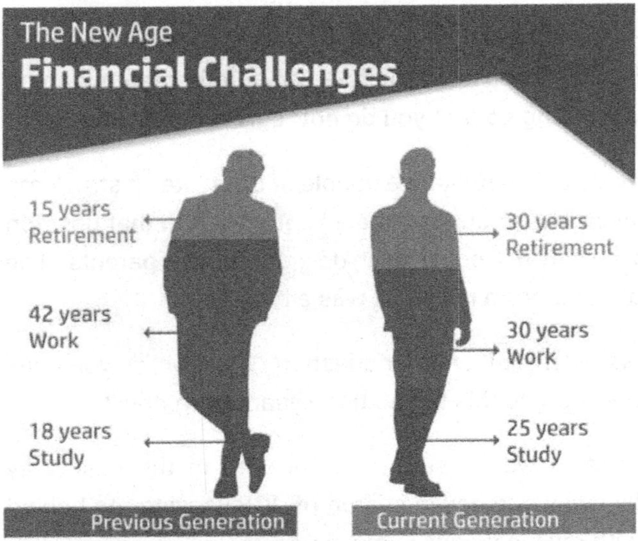

As compared to our previous generation, our number of working years has shrunk and number of years after retirement has gone up due to higher life expectancy

I would sincerely urge that: we must prioritise our Retirement Planning – Financial Freedom planning. Most of us get caught in our day to day living fight and tend to delay it and by the time we realise it's too late. Further today's generation Financial Challenge is that all aspire to take early retirement but we couldn't.

Hence, Retirement planning is very critical and we should save from the day we get our first salary or income cheque.

Financial Freedom Goal - Retirement Planning:

One thing we should remember for ever that – We will get loan for all needs such as car, home, consumer durables etc. But no one give loan to us to fund our Retirement. Hence we need to plan our Retirement planning very effectively. And starting early is the secret to it as illustrated in previous chapter with Ram & Shyam examples.

Mr Mitra

Your Retirement Planning

Current age	35 Years
Retirement age	58 Years
Life expectance (In Year)	80 Years
Current monthly expenses	Rs. 35,000.00
Inflation	5%
Post retirement inflation	4%
Post retirement risk free rate of return	4%
Existing investment	Rs. 10,00,000.00
Return On existing investment	8%
Return On new investment	9%

Based on above assumptions you shall receive

Monthly expense at a time of retirement	Rs. 1,07,503.00
Yearly expense at a time of retirement	Rs. 12,90,036.00
Future value of current investment	Rs. 58,71,463.65
Corpus required at a time of retirement	Rs. 225,09,328.35
Option 1	
Lumpsum Investment require to achieve goal	Rs. 31,01,366.45
Option 2	
SIP require to achive goal	Rs. 25,738.95

The above example clearly reveals that if Mitra needs to maintain the same life style as he is maintain now: he need to save INR 21,000 per month towards his Financial Freedom kitty.

Retirement Planning should start from the day we receive our first pay cheque

Key Takeaways:

....

....

....

....

Chapter 17

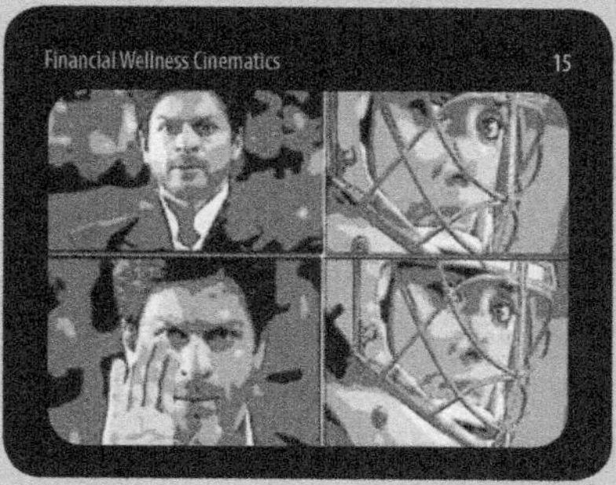

Chak De India - Rebalancing Strategy

All of you can recall in the movie the last penalty shoot out in the Hockey finals between in India & Australia. Looking at the foot movement coach could identy that stiker will hit the ball at the center and he is simply preying that goal keeper should look at her once. As the eyes of goal keeper meets the coach he simply raises his hand guiding her to stand at the center. As the coach stratagise match winning strategy before every match: similarly an Advisor should do Portfolio Rebalancing at regular intervels depending upon the market movement.

Volatility Game: Rebalancing Strategy

I have talked about the inspiring movie *One Idiot*, taken you through the subjects of Power of Compounding, spoken about Asset Allocation and expounded on the virtues of Energy Consciousness. And now, I shall steer my narrative in the direction of Volatility Game, a game that has been recognised and awarded by **The Economic Times** and **Wealth Forum**. It is created by my mentor Mr. Kanak Jain and along with this has created dozens of game on Financial Planning.

Every financial trainer has a USP, and for us it is this Volatility Game. We have conducted over 100 times in the past 2 years. It is a unique game as it merges facts with fun, entertainment with education, and knowledge with thrill. The game is software, one of our intellectual properties which throw up excellent and new investment possibilities every time we begin a fresh game.

One major irony today is that investors are unable to strike the right balance between the various sentiments of attachment, greed, risk and fear. More often than not, they invest in assets when the prices are nearing the peak or at the peak or are at high risk. This can be corrected by reorganising your strategy using what we term as the Re-balancing Strategy.

Re-balancing Strategy and various Volatility Games help the investors (and potential investors) to figure out the best strategies and to decide whether to buy, to hold or to sell a particular asset class. The twin combination of Volatility Games and Rebalancing Strategy ensures a much more prudent mode of asset allocation and thus enables a stronger portfolio that offers enhanced returns.

It was one such occasion at a session I was conducting in New Delhi. My pep-talk had made them abuzz, and each one of them was waiting for the Volatility Game to begin. It is a screen-based game and has a flashy Casino-type look. As I logged into the software and began the game, the Casino-like image popped up on the screen with a popping sound. It was followed immediately by the sound of a slotting machine that obviously turns the audience on, making each one of them look forward to it with eager anticipation.

"I really loved the game," said Miss Sneha. Another member named Harish quipped, "This is really interesting, Sir and I love the fact that it has made financial education so simple." Another person named Arijit commented in a half-laughing way, "I wish we had such games to teach us mathematics back in our school days."

Besides they were pretty amazed that a subject like Finance could be so fun. Considered as a serious topic, people find it amusing that Finance can be so simplified through the help of such games. My good friend Mr. Ashish is a great fan of the game and uses the game and the P/E scale to make buying, selling and holding decisions.

He told me over the phone last day, "This game is really unique, probably one of a kind. It teaches me how to do Portfolio Rebalancing based upon parameters like P/E ratio and Market Cap to MG Ratio."

So, see my friends, Rebalancing is a strategy that helps in making your earnings regular and consistent. This strategy executes the idea of "Buy low and sell high."

Yes, each and every investor has a wish to buy low and sell high. But any individual investor is controlled by two contradictory emotions- the emotion of "Greed" and the emotion of "Fear". Yes, most of the people make losses and quit investments because they are unable to control these two emotions while investing. As the investment Guru Warren Buffet says –**"Buy when others are fearful and sell when others are greedy".**

The conclusion is that whenever the Sensex/nifty valuation become overvalued and reaches the bubble zone, it falls. The strategy here is to reduce the exposure to equity and increase debt in your portfolio. This is a strategy where you sell when P/E multiple is high or at bubble zone. And buy when the valuation of market P/E multiple is low. A simple PE scale is presented below for reference.

P/E Scale of India:

Average Returns	CAGR		
PE	**1 Year**	**3 Year**	**5 Year**
<14	60.23%	51.64%	31.41%
14-16	36.24%	43.59%	33.32%
16-18	21.94%	25.18%	21.48%
18-20	10.75%	17.60%	14.94%
20-22	4.11%	9.30%	9.89%
22-24	-8.40%	1.35%	9.99%
24+	-30.60%	-7.37%	4.29%

DalalStreetBulls

P/E denotes whether the market price of equity is justified in terms of the profitability of the Company. Another crucial parameter is P/B which denotes whether the market price is justified in terms of the Company's Net Assets or Net Worth.

Another observation from the above P/E Scale is that the market remains in the region of 14 to 22 PE for more than 70% of the time. Below 14x P/E market has gone only 15% of the occasion and above 22xP/E it has gone on only15% of the occasion.

As above, it is also suggested that the equity allocation of during the P/E level below 14x should be up to 80% or more. Equity allocation in the region of 14x-22x P/E suggested is between 40-50% depending on the levels. And finally the P/E level above 22x (which is more or less a bubble zone) should have equity below 20% in portfolio.

So, managing volatility is the key to wealth creation.

Portfolio rebalancing is must to generate consistant returns

Key Takeaways:

....

....

....

....

Chapter 18

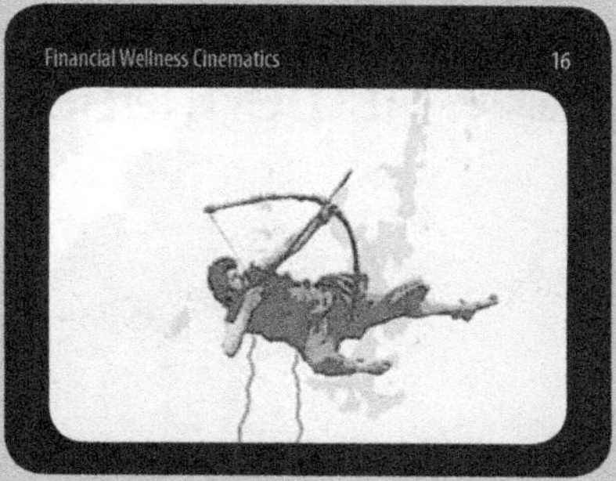

Bahubali: The Fearless Investor

Correction is Temporary and growth is Permanent
Be fearless like Bahubali ; Don't be greedy like Bhallaldev
(Brother of Bahubali)

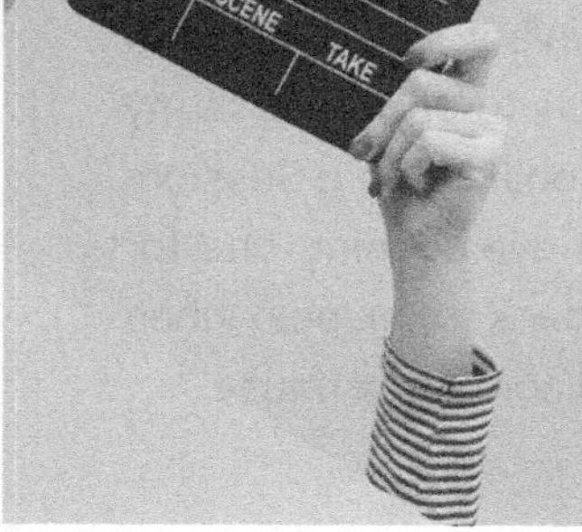

The Sequel blockbuster teaches us to be fearless during all circumstances (like Bahubali the actor) and not be greedy like Bhallaldev (Brother of Bahubali)

COVID-19 crisis and the ongoing lockdown period have given all of us a fresh perspective towards life. This is a phase where one can take a breather, reflect on life and take firmer future decisions. This period also provided me a fascinating chance to engage with 300-odd employees of Xorient Technologies over Zoom.

I remember I was a bit nervous as I sat down before the laptop in my drawing room, not sure if I would be able to drive across my plans related to Financial Wellness over an online Zoom Session. However, the session turned out to be an eye-opening one for many of us. This period also helped us go back to the past when the world (or the stock market) had indeed come to a pause.

The chief agenda of my session was this- **"Correction is Temporary and growth is permanent. Present Correction seems like a big problem and all past correction seems to us a lost opportunity."**

I began my session my asking them "How many of you have experienced a Roller Coaster Ride: Few replied in Chat Box YES!! So I asked the candidate to unmute himself and share his experience:

He Replied "Once the roller coaster goes up we are thrilled and our excitement goes up and when it does down we feel nervous!! All other people must be thinking that how could market be linked with roller coaster:

Same is with Market: When market goes up we are excited and when it falls we feel scared. Market is just like a roller coaster ride...

When Rollercoaster goes down: do we open our seat belt and jump off!! No If we do so we know the repercussions.

Similarly when market also goes down, if we sell our holdings we will be converting our paper loss into actual loss.

Thus friends: market goes through its own ups and down and we need to simply ride the volatility and focus towards our end goal.

For example, if a person has invested for his child education and needs money after 10 years he should not be worried with such volatility now as because money is required after 10 year. Moreover, If he has done a SIP he should rather be very happy because more units would have been accumulating at a lower price.

This roller coaster experience sets as a stepping stone to my session.

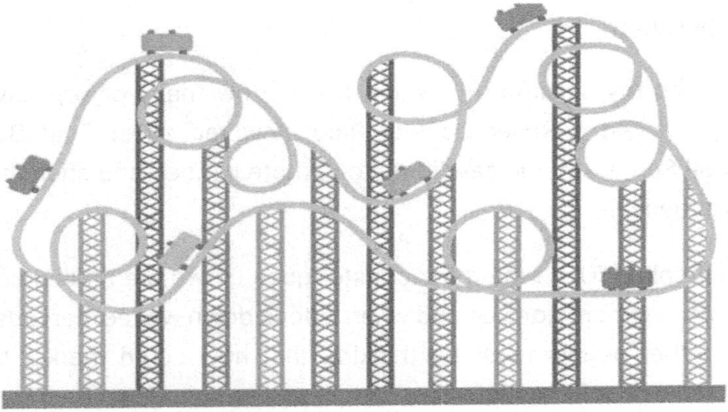

Let's learn from History!!

Let us go back to the Harshad Mehta scam of 1992. It rattled the Indian Stock Market, making the SENSEX crash down by 54% in just one year. However, those who had the foresight to judge the future began to invest money in the market. And they were rewarded soon as SENSEX recovered by 127% in 1.5 years.

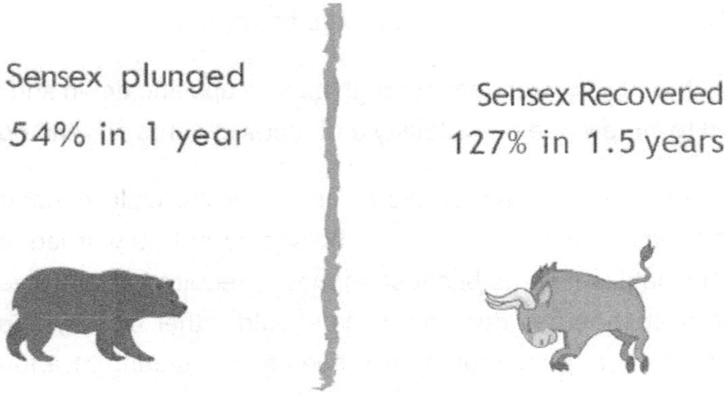

During the 1996 Asian Crisis, the SENSEX plunged 40% in 4 years but it recovered by 115% in 1 year. The Lehman Brothers crisis of

2008 again proved that the market will surely bounce back and those who have the patience and vision actually made a lump sum from it. SENSEX had dropped down by 61% that time in 1 year but the comeback was steep at 157% in 1.5 years.

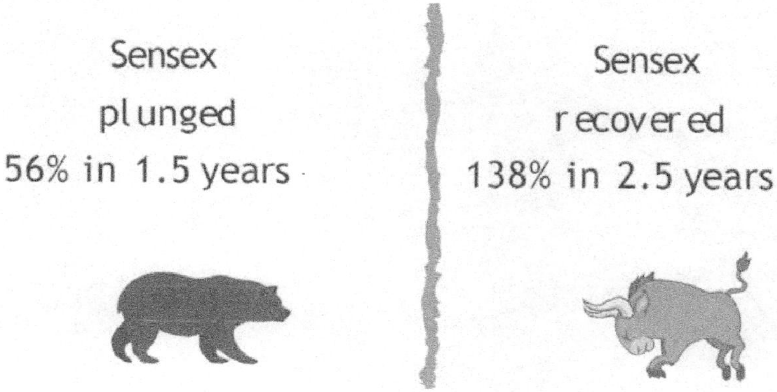

"It is not just the stock market," as I said to my audience on the Zoom session. "It is the world in general that knows how to bounce back. The World War 1 and 2 are perfect examples," I cited. "Can anyone point out any health hazard from which the world recovered and took a U-turn," I tossed a question to my virtual audience.

"The Spanish Flu, Sir", answered a very young man named Arun Mohta. "Nearly 5 million people died all over the world between 1919 and 1922 during the Spanish Flu," he informed.

I appreciated his remark. It was true. Currently, we are facing a very similar episode of viral infection all over the planet but, like the Spanish Flu, this too will go. Very soon, we will be talking about the Corona Virus in the past tense.

The chart below clearly depicts that we have gone through many health crises but if we look at last 20 year graph: market has delivered 12% plus CAGR return up till March.

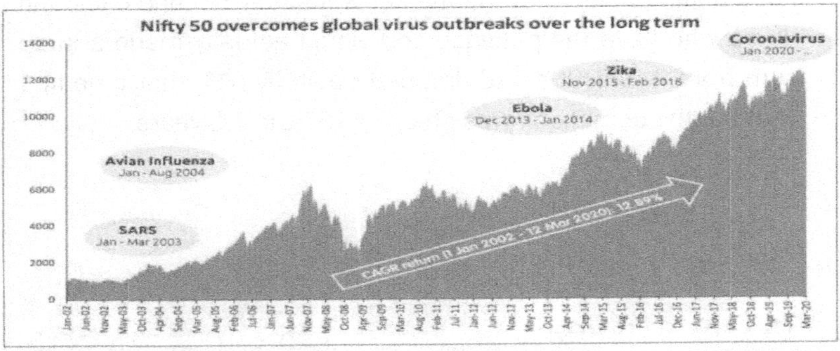

Virus	Outbreak Period	Nifty 50 returns (Absolute)	
		During Outbreak	After 1 year
SARS	Jan – Mar 2003	-11.08%	**80.85%**
Avian Influenza	Jan – Aug 2004	-14.67%	**46.14%**
Ebola	Dec 2013 – Jan 2014	-1.40%	**44.80%**
Zika	Nov 2015 – Feb 2016	-13.37%	**27.09%**
Coronavirus	Jan 2020 –...	-21.28%*	?

So that brings us to the thought of the day- **Is the present market situation a decent time to invest?** When we look at the past events, many of us do realise that those were lost opportunities when risk-averse investors withdrew their money and later regretted not having reinvested.

The Zoom session, made further engaging with Polls and Quiz Questions, turned out to be an incredible success. Mr. Bala, an MBA from a premiere business school, later contacted me and showed a keen interest in financial planning. Our PPTs had convinced many others that Financial Wellness is as important as Physical or Mental Wellness.

It is a human psychology to become fearful, go into a shell and withdraw all funds from the market (even at a loss) at this time. But those who learn from the past opt to go for safer investment modes like SIPs so that the current opportunity does not become another lost opportunity.

This again reminds me of legendary advice from the legend!

Be greedy when others are fearful, and be fearful when others are greedy. "Mr. Warren Buffett"

It is easy to read loud!! But when it comes to practise it is very difficult to practise yourself!! Thus there is need of a Financial Advisor who would not only guide us in terms of selection of right product but also help us in managing our Behaviour.

After all, as is rightly said, 'Correction is Temporary, while Growth is Permanent.'

Manage your greed and fear while investing

Key Takeaways:

....

....

....

....

Chapter 19

Dil Chahta Hai

Where we usually Invest & where should we actually Invest...

Where we Invest & where should we actually Invest:

Just like Aakash (Aamir) finally became serious about what his (Dil) heart really desires (chahta hai), and invested his efforts into the things around him (his love, his friends) instead of chasing happiness in external world, similarly when it comes to investment all ideas and products are around us but we keep running after distant objects and once we realise its late.

This story goes back to the day I landed up at a Pune Bajaj Auto Plant with my friend Piyush Rakhecha. We were slated to conduct a session on Financial Wellness with young engineer graduates as a part of their induction programme. What is intriguing about this day is how I was able to drive home a very interesting point. Consumerism has taken over this world. We are all consumers but perhaps what we fail to note is that the products that we consume are the products that we can earn from.

As we began running slides, I came to the slide which depicts our day long journey and connects with our consumption story.

This is how we start our days. Most of us quit our beds, say, around 6 am and immediately check our WhatsApp for texts and missed calls, if any. For many of us, we need an Airtel or a Jio or a Vodafone network's service much before heading to the washroom. Strange, but true!

At around 7 am, say, we brush our teeth and once again we lean on a Pepsodent or a Colgate to see us through. At 8 am, we sit down to sip a steaming cup of hot Tata tea with some mouth-watering ITC biscuits. At 9 am, we drive to the office in a Maruti car or in a Bajaj scooter. At 10 am, we log in to our office duties we use Google, Microsoft Office and instantly take software assistance of a package made by Infosys or TCS.

At 11 am, maybe, we get your salary credited in your Kotak Bank. At 12, we might just receive an SMS of our loan clearance from HDFC bank. At 1 pm, our staffs use Hero Honda bikes to make some deliveries.

The moment the Hero Bike logo came up on the screen, the youngistan erupted in mild protest, "Sir, it should be Bajaj, not Hero. You are in our Plant, sir."

They were basically pulling my legs. I chuckled in acknowledgement of their quick observation and said, "Point noted, my dear friends. We will amend it next time."

And we began proceeding with the next set of images.

At 2 pm, we head out for lunch and use ICICI ATM card to withdraw cash. At 3 pm, maybe we find our secretary taking delivery of a product ordered from Amazon. Around 4 pm we gaze out of office through the windows built of Tata Steel. Many of you are whizzing past the flyover in the evening traffic of 5 pm. That flyover, obviously, is an invention of L & T.

Many of us, my dear readers, enjoy Nestle coffee at around 6 pm with our pals and colleagues. As we head back to our home at 7 pm, we use the street lights which could be manufactured from Philips. Back in our drawing room at 8, we relax and rejuvenate and let the Bajaj fan do its job and dry off our sweat.

At 9 pm, our parents may a take their diabetes pills that could be manufactured by Divis Laboratories and at 10 pm, we are on the dinner table with Britannia cheese or ITC Ashirwad aata. At 11 pm, we switch on the AC and retire to bed.

After running the above slide, I quizzed my audience. “Tell me, what did I just show you?”

They were slightly taken aback by this question but they gave some smart answers. Some said, ”You showed us, Sir, that we are spending throughout the day.” We all laughed.

Others replied, “I am making other people rich.” I smiled.

One smart young guy Mr. Pulkit replied, “Sir, It is our Stock Portfolio you are showing us.”- I replied, “Bang on.”

I then explained, “Yes my dear friends, what I have just displayed, it could be your stock or Mutual fund portfolio. Our investment should go into these stocks which we or people around us are consuming.

If we ensure this simple strategy, then in my view we really don’t need expert opinions, and we can make decent money from the market.

They all were smiling. They had understood, and understood well.

I remember, I also pointed this out to my father-in-law a few days back, he made a very witty remark. He said, "Most of the companies will sleep if we stop sleeping." It is true. Our sleep and waking up cycle revolves around multiple brands of tea, biscuits, mobile phone networks, Air-conditioners and something as small as a GoodNight mosquito repellent.

I mulled over his statement and replied to my father-in-law, "We spend a lot over these brands. In fact, every moment we are doing an activity, which is basically throughout the day, we are spending on one such company. Isn't it high time that we earn back from them?"

"How," he quipped, his interest level going up.

"By investing," I replied coolly. "The products are not going to go anywhere till human settlement exists. These companies are going to be there even after many of us die. Look at Tata, it is existing since much before I or you were born."

"So?" he answered back.

"So this, ideally we should invest in companies which are consumed by people around us. It is high time we earn from the sources where we spend." And saying this and leaving him a bit overwhelmed, I bade him goodnight and left the room.

The crux of the matter, my friends, is that our common everyday life (no matter how boring it be) is full of opportunities. We just need to open our eyes and look around. There is an opportunity to earn in every single expenditure we make.

Wake up, smell that *Tata Tea* and open an SIP.

List down what
perople are
consuming around us

Key
Takeaways:

....

....

....

....

Chapter 20

Bazaar: Learning the rules of the Financial Bazaar

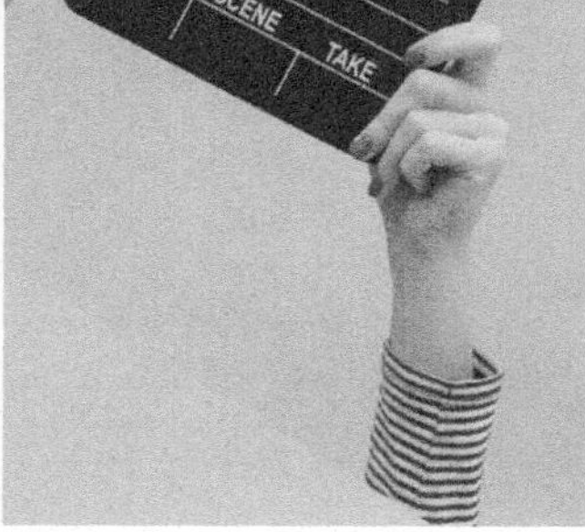

"In Financial Bazaar
- Dont's are more
Important than Do's ...

Do's and Don'ts of Investments:

I am grateful to the head of Kone Elevators in Ranchi who made a very wise statement at the end of a Financial Wellness session that proved to be an eye-opener for many of us. He simply said, in his deep guttural voice, "I have understood Saurabh what you explained and your session was indeed a beautiful one. But when it comes to investing, *the Don'ts are more important than the Do's."*

I gaped at him, the truth sitting wide in his eyes. I understood the depth in his statement, something that I too knew but had been overlooking for a long time.

"Why don't you do a session on the wrong strategies of investing," he added and encouraged me to chalk out a few guidelines for the young investors. I was pretty much bowled over the maturity shown by Mr. Avdhesh Kumar a young manager and dedicate this article to the ingenious statement he made that day.

Here, this image will serve as a good illustration on what I will endeavour to say today. Many people, especially the young enthusiastic investors, make hurried decisions especially during volatile market conditions. These decisions often become a point of regret in a few months.

Mutual Funds, that are a combined portfolio of stocks, securities and bonds, become a safer place to park your fund as they do not necessitate 24/7 monitoring. So, compared to equity shares, mutual funds offer you that cushion of safety in the short as well as in the long run.

Nonetheless, a few tips every investor should keep in mind are as follows:

1] **Be patient and don't sell off low performers in a hurry**: We should wait for at least a year before selling the low performers off. Many funds offer negligible or even negative return in the short run but make up for it and bring a handsome profit in the mid-to-long run.

2] **In a downturn, don't sell everything off**: Mutual funds, as mentioned earlier, are managed by professional stock market analysts and fund managers with years of investment experience under their belts. In tough economic times, they take proactive measures to minimize the impact of the downturn on their portfolios, like switching sectors or specific stocks to minimize losses.

I remember telling my 22-year cousin Harsh once, "One problem with young people is that they depend a lot on their gut feeling instead of the advice given by a trained professional. Decisions made based on gut feelings are signs of financial immaturity and should be avoided."

3] **Avoid putting your money into stock market bubbles**: When a stock or a sector bubbles based on rumours without having a long-term fundamentals, people queue up to buy it in bulk. But these are market bubbles and are often deceptive. 'A bubble in a stock or a sector that appears to grow suddenly and, therefore, is a huge temptation especially for a child investor. But soon enough, they burst and those who have invested in bulk often stand to lose,' I told Harsh later that day.

4] **Don't park your funds based on short term performance**: The performance of any Mutual Fund must be observed and analysed over a period of 1-5 years, and not based on a few weeks or months. This is crucial. Look at CONSISTENCY, don't get distracted by market MOVEMENTS.

5] **Don't put all money in one fund**: My friend Pratik, who has been investing since he was in college with me, often makes simple but deep statements. He had said, as we were sitting with Samosa and a cup of coffee under the blazing sunlight in the canteen of St. Xavier's College, "My friend, we should never put all our eggs in one basket. Never invest more than 30% of your total investment in one fund."

I still remember that statement even after 14 years.

Example- If you have Rs 50,000 to invest. Don't invest more than Rs 15,000 (30% of 50,000) in one fund.

As Warren Buffet had said, "Diversification is a protection against ignorance."

So you see, diversification is the key but pick your funds after a careful analysis of the long-term market and avoid common mistakes.

Finincial Wellness Session conducted at KONE Elevators Ranchi Office

Dont's are more important than Do's

Key Takeaways:

....

....

....

....

Chapter 21

PK: Our Behaviour Guru and Behaviour Finance

Humka laagat hai bhagwan se baat kare ka communication system is gola ka total lul ho chuka hai".

English translation – "The communication system of this planet for talking to God ... has become totally useless ".

We are simply following what others are doing instead of doing our Research towards what is right or wrong!!

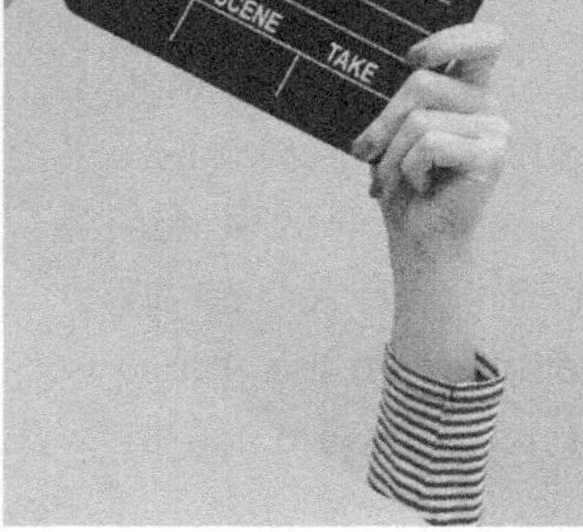

Investment Behaviour and how it matters in Financial World:

Nick Murray once said, "Wealth is not only determined by investment performance but by investor behaviour."

The above quotation clearly reveals the significance of behaviour Finance in our investment strategy. Many of us think that financial market is all out Valuations, ratios, Trends etc. But my dear friends our behaviour & psychology is a key determinant towards Wealth Creation.

In the month of May 2020, I got an opportunity to do a zoom session exclusively on Behaviour Finance with a large conglomerate Lafarge Holchim. In recent months, I focus a lot on this term called Investment Behaviour, and the time was raw to bring that topic out in the open.

Return is determined primarily by our behaviour. To prove that a study was done on behaviour finance and this study is known as a behaviour gap study. Research was done in United States whereby they have taken the return of all the investors for last 30 years of all their folios. What the study revealed is that the actual return which the market gave was approximately was close to

10%, CAGR but on an average, the investor got only 6% return.

So, why did this gap of 4% exist? The answer, my friends, is because of Investor Behaviour.

Mr. Anil Agarwal, one of the participants at the session, said, "Isn't it related to the Investor's Psychology?"

I nodded my head appreciatively, and replied "The psychology of an average investor is that money should be invested when the market is experiencing a boom phase or period. They panic when the market goes down and take out all the money which, in my opinion, reflects the typical Investment Behaviour. During consolidation phase when the market is flat, the investor reels in confusion, not knowing whether to invest more or to withdraw his/her existing investments. It is here that different people make different choices, mainly governed by their own investment behaviour and risk-taking appetite."

I adjusted my mike a bit and added, "This is Behavioural Bias. People behave in a biased way, and not uniformly. But overall, on an average, they invest during boom and withdraw during a slump period. This leads to less-than-expected returns." In other words, Investment Behaviour is the key determinant to wealth creation. **As we proceed ahead and take poll by asking one common question:**

Our investment choices are determined by what is happening around us. Investors tend to time the market by trying to find the sweet spots during market movements.

Even when investment performance is good, a large number of studies have suggested that investor returns have been less than investment returns. This happens primarily because of irrational investor behavior.

"Which is the oldest stock exchange in the world?" And we toss a few options at them viz.

1. **Amsterdam**
2. **London**
3. **New York**
4. **Bombay**

Most of the time the answer that we get from the audience is either London, New York or Bombay but the correct answer is Amsterdam. But why 90% of the people say the other ones because they **"felt", so. This** biasness is called as an **overconfidence bias** which is there within all of us and first thing which an investor should do is to try to reduce such overconfidence bias. It exists within all of us to a certain degree. All of us are just one Google away from finding out the correct answer. **Yet, most of us are driven by our inner instincts or feelings.**

The Financial market too functions in this manner, but investors should not take decisions based on gut feelings. The correct thing is market study, using analytical tools and obviously reviewing on expert advice.

We often sell as we 'feel' that the market has reached its peak, or we buy a stock 'feeling' that the correction in the stock is over and we should pump our money in that stock.

Patience and waiting, here, becomes the key, as pointed out by the great finance masters.

The big money is not in Buying and selling... But in waiting

– Charlie Munger

It is here that I offered a story of a Football Match:

"During a penalty shootout in Football, the goalkeeper usually jumps to the right or to the left. Research, however, says that the ideal strategy would be to remain at the centre. Yet the goalkeeper goes by his gut feeling and takes a biased decision-either preferring his right or his left. This, my dear friends, is called Action Biasness. It exists in the Financial Market too, where we either buy or sell during a penalty shootout-like market phase. But, as Mr. Warren Buffet, says that waiting or remaining at the centre (neither buying nor selling) may just be the right

The Stock Market
is a wonderfully
efficient mechanism
for transferring
wealth from the
Impatient to patient

- Warren Buffett

strategy in such times. Not always, but more often than not."

Mr. Vikash who was keenly following the session said, "It means that we should not be tempted to take decisions based on our instinctive feeling during volatile market situations, right?"

He had got the drift of the matter, alright. I smiled at him encouragingly and nodded my head.

Then I began with my second story.

"A man decided to reach the top of a mountain, All the people standing below started shouting that it's impossible, it's...... impossible. Yet the man reached the top."

I paused and asked the question,

"How did he reach? Someone answered that he was determined! Another said that he was focussed towards his goal.

I remember a smart lady named Ankita, had answered, "He was deaf."

Yes!! He was indeed deaf and he thought that everyone was encouraging him to reach the top. He could reach the top because he could not listen to the negative voices around. !! Similarly, as an investor, if you want to create wealth you need to learn to ignore the voices. Dont listen to what newspaper headlines have to say about the market. Newspaper headlines can only tell you about yesterday and your portfolio return is based on tomorrow. **I think that the worst mistake you can make in stocks to buy or sell based on current headlines.** People who think that they can predict the short-term movement of the stock market or those who listen to other people who talk about timing of the market are making a big blunder. DO your own home work and invest your money wisely.

Mr. Vineet another participant expressed that he is an active trader but could not make much wealth as the profit he made in one share was compensated by the loss he incurred in the other. After listening to our speech above, he was really taken aback. It was certainly an eye-opening session for him. Later, he thanked us and made a resolution that he would not only invest by watching television & would adopt a goal-based financial plan towards long term wealth creation.

Are you the next Vineet!

Dear Readers: Behaviour Finance is a vast ocean all of has some of the other biasness within us. It is not possible to overcome all but we should try and reduce such biasness to improve our investment decisions.

Overall, Investment Behaviour is the key to successful planning. As an investor, therefore, you need to keep this aspect in mind.

A thank you note being shared by HR manager of LafargeHolcim

LafargeHolcim

THANK YOU

Thank you So Much Sourabh for your Time invested in the conducting a webinar on Financial Wellness

The Session was rich on content and our participants had a lot to take away .

The Total Participation was 65 employees ☺

Thank you once again for your efforts and time.

Best Regards
Team HR

Our behaviour is a key determinant factor towards our wealth creation

Key Takeaways:

....

....

....

....

Chapter 22

VOLATILITY COACHES OF INDIA

Cinematic Review.

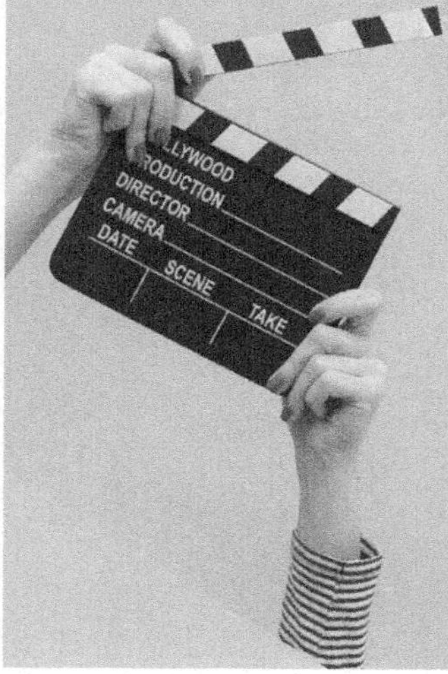

Lets Summarise the learning My experience & story as an advisor got published in The Economic Times with some top advisors of India.

THE ECONOMIC TIMES
PRESENTATION

VOLATILITY COACHES OF INDIA

SOURABH JAIN, Kolkata

Most of the time people understand mutual fund as an only equity investments. But mutual fund is the only asset class which provides option to invest in diversified product basket such as equity, debt, hybrid, arbitrage, gold etc. From past experience, I have learnt adding fixed income product in client portfolio and specially any lump sum allocation should go to debt and depending upon the market trend, rebalance strategy should be adopted to make advantage of equity price movement. I am happy to do such portfolio allocation for a senior citizen client. All his investments were deployed into the equity. Considering his age, we did 80:20 Debt: Equity allocation in the portfolio which ensures capital protection plus stable return. Further, we activated Systematic Withdrawal Plan (SWP) which offers regular monthly income to the client from debt portion. Therefore, fixed income fund should form part of the every investor's portfolio and allocation should be tuned depending upon client's risk profile and age.

Summary of Key Take Away:

Final Words: As I sit down to summarise the key findings, here is what I have on my paper:

- ***Have Positive Attitude about money***
- ***Power of Compounding & benefits of starting early***
- ***Buy only plain Vanilla - Term Insurance***
- ***Health Insurance Coverage – as per need***
- ***Emergency Fund Corpus***
- ***Goal based Financial Planning***
- ***Diversify and create a decent pool of portfolio***
- ***Take help of a financial expert or advisor (don't go by gut feeling)***
- ***Be fearless at times but do not take a rash decision***
- ***And above all, always be ready to learn***

I would suggest you all to collate your take away from each chapter and then draw your own Financial Pyramid. It will definitely enlighten us to fix up some blind spots in our Financial Planning which can be rectified.

Friends, I am happy to share that:

Our Organisation Suskan Consultants Pvt Ltd was recognized as the most Preferred Financial Wellness Partner during the **HR Sampark Wellness Conclave on Feb 2020 at HHI kolkata. HR Sampark is a Trust**

Mr. Debargha Deb HR Dabur East India, Mr. RJ Rakesh Mr. Saurabh Jain (CIO Suskan Consultants) & Mr. Ajit Menon, CEO PGIM Indian Mutual Fund (From Left to Right)

As I put down my pen, I see a huge change come over me. It has been an enlightening journey, writing this book. I feel fulfilled in the process and I am thankful to my friends, well-wishers and readers for lending me their time and being patient with me. I would like to make an appeal to all of you to kindly overlook any mistake I may have made while writing this book. Though I have tried my best to avoid any error, I am sure you all will be good enough to ignore any error that may have escaped my attention.

Failing to plan is planning to Fail - Kick start your Financial Planning Journey

Key Takeaways:

....

....

....

....

ACKNOWLEDGEMENT

EDITOR

SOURABH JAIN

PUBLICATION DESIGN

NAINA BAINDUR - SAIMAA

MARKETING

PENMAN BOOKS

EDITORIAL ENQUIRIES

SOURABH@ASKSUSKAN.COM

PUBLISHED & DISTRIBUTED BY

PENMAN BOOKS

WITH SPECIAL THANK TO

KANAK JAIN

RITESH AGARWAL

KHUSHBOO JAIN

Made in the USA
Monee, IL
05 November 2026

67380081R00100